ESSENTIAL GUIDE *to* BOATING

BOATING LESSONS
YOU'LL NEVER FORGET

SAFETY, EMERGENCY AND SURVIVAL TECHNIQUES
FROM REAL-LIFE DISASTER STORIES

skills institute press

*Distributed By
Fox Chapel Publishing*

FOX CHAPEL
PUBLISHING

© 2012 by Skills Institute Press LLC
"Essential Guide to Boating" series trademark of Skills Institute Press
Published and distributed in North America by Fox Chapel Publishing Company, Inc., East
Petersburg, PA.

Boating Lessons You'll Never Forget is an original work, first published in 2012.

Portions of text and art previously published by and reproduced under license with Direct
Holdings Americas Inc.

ISBN: 978-1-56523-590-8

Library of Congress Cataloging-in-Publication Data

Boating lessons you'll never forget : safety, emergency and survival techniques from real-life
disaster stories.
     p. cm. -- (Essential guide to boating)
Includes index.
 Summary: "Not a guide book, but a great read. Real life disasters and how they lived to tell
the stories fill the pages of this book. Everything from sperm whales biting a hole in a hull and
escaping in a rubber dinghy while your boat goes down in the Pacific to running ashore on rocky
shoals. Also includes tips on how to survive when the worst happens"-- Provided by publisher.
 ISBN 978-1-56523-590-8 (pbk.)
 1. Boats and boating--Safety measures.
GV775.B555 2011
797.10289--dc22
                              2011013454

To learn more about the other great books from Fox Chapel Publishing,
or to find a retailer near you, call toll-free 800-457-9112 or visit us at
www.FoxChapelPublishing.com.

Note to Authors: We are always looking for talented authors to write new books. Please send a
brief letter describing your idea to
Acquisition Editor, 1970 Broad Street, East Petersburg, PA 17520.

Printed in China
First printing

Table of Contents

Introduction 6

Chapter 1: Wind and Waves 8

Wind Patterns 12

Fighting Fires Afloat 16

Hazard in the Galley 18

Fuel and Engine Fires 20

Riding Out the Storm 24

Reading the Weather 26

How Weather Works 28

Signs in the Sky 32

Stormy Weather 34

Fear Was Our Constant Companion . . 36

Man Overboard 38

Search and Pickup 40

Chapter 2: Animal Encounters . . . 42

Attacked by a Great White 44

Signaling for Help 50

Radio Distress Calls 51

Abandoning Ship 56

Rescue by Air 64

Chapter 3: Avoiding the Rocks . . . 68

Lost at Sea 70

A Revealing Perspective 78

The Underwater Terrain 81

Clear Warnings of Shoal Waters 83

Symbols for Landmarks 86

A Mariner's Match-up 88

The Rules of The Road 90

Collision Courses: Power 92

Collision Courses: Sail 94

Intrusions on the Fairway 97

Narrow Passages 100

Fog and Distress Signals 102

Lights on Inland Waters 104

International Lights 106

Changing Look of Lights 109

Inland Fishing and Towing 110

Offshore Fishing and Towing 110

Lights for Anchoring and Distress . . 112

Chapter 4: Power and Safety 114

Powerboat Preparations 118

Essential Safety Gear 120

Starting the Engine 122

Preparing a Sailboat 126

Restoring Power 130

Steering Failure 133

Repairing the Rig 135

Aid for an Upset 138

Index 140

What You
Can Learn

Wind and Waves, page 8

Violent weather can assail boaters in any sea,
lake, or river, but by learning to watch for
signs and knowing how to deal with weather
as it occurs, boaters can ride out any storm.

Animal Encounters, page 42

Unexpected calamity can occur when boaters
underestimate the residents of the sea.
Whether stove in by a shark or a breaching
whale, a boater needs to be prepared to repair
or evacuate.

Avoiding the Rocks, page 68

Learning to read charts and to understand

water will keep boaters in safe waters.

Power and Safety, page 114

Before heading out on the water, every skipper

should take precautions to ensure the safety

and well-being of his boat and its passengers.

Introduction

Withstanding the Sea's Malice

Most of the sailors who go out onto the oceans of the world reach their destinations with no serious mishap and much satisfaction. Given a sturdy boat, properly equipped, an experienced mariner can ride out the most savage conditions of wind and sea, as demonstrated by the vessel at right, slogging along in gale-force winds off Cape Horn. Its skipper, the British mariner Sir Francis Chichester, was making his singlehanded circumnavigation of the globe, and had chosen the difficult route around the Horn for the very challenge it would provide. "I hate being frightened," he said later, "but, even more, I detest being prevented by fright."

But the sea can be an infinitely treacherous and unforgiving mistress, and on occasion it will lash out in such wildly unpredictable ways that neither the most careful planning nor the most skillful seamanship will serve to withstand it. Who would expect, for example, that a freak wave, tall as a seven-story building, would suddenly rise behind his boat and flip it transom over mast in a catastrophic somersault? Or that a 40-ton right whale would breach and land on a nearby sailboat? Or that an enormous shark would mistake his boat for another fish and ram a hole through its bottom? Yet these astounding mishaps, and others like them, do in fact occur, as the stories on the following pages testify. Just as astounding, the victims have survived to tell about them. Many of us caught Today® in December 2010 as Amanda Thorns recounted the horror of losing her father overboard during a nor'easter and fashioning a new mast and sail to limp home.

Each of the survivors owed his or her life to a combination of remarkably good seamanship, ingenuity, and coolness under fire. Though none of the particular disasters could have been foreseen, each person was, in a sense, prepared to meet it. For in every case, the victim possessed reserves of know-how and fortitude that allowed him or her to deal with the crisis at hand. And their stories hold lessons in survival for anyone—from a round-the-world voyager to a family on an offshore weekend—who may find themselves in deep trouble at sea.

Francis Chichester's *Gypsy Moth IV* braves the violent seas off Cape Horn in 1967; a storm jib steadies the boat and maintains steerageway. Six hours after this photograph was taken, the wind blew up to 85 knots. But the 65-year-old lone mariner and his vessel rode out the tempest without needing so much as a single adjustment of sail.

CHAPTER 1:
Wind and Waves

by Erroll Bruce

The sea taught me a tough lesson about preparedness when I was only 19. I anticipated no trouble when I set out to cruise the China coast with four friends in a borrowed ketch, the 35-foot *Tavy II*. So intense was my enjoyment of the balmy first night of the cruise that I scarcely left the deck. The dawn was beautiful, too. After that I went below for some sleep. Soon I awoke, sensing a change in conditions. The boat was pitching to a new swell from the east, while the wind held steady from the south. I tapped the barometer; it showed no change. But somehow the sky looked different, and an hour later the barometer showed a distinct drop. Such signs could mean that a typhoon—the common Pacific term for a hurricane—was forming somewhere in the China Sea.

I had never experienced a typhoon, but I knew that if there were any chance of meeting one, no sane seaman would willingly remain on open water. We turned around to run back to Hong Kong. "Secure for heavy weather," I told the other lads, "and get out that sea anchor from the forepeak." Our sea anchor was an open-ended canvas cone attached by a bridle to a line. It could be trailed out from one end of the boat or the other to slow down the vessel and keep the bow or stern to the wind.

The wind increased, as did our speed, and before the weather became too threatening we closed on Tathong Point at the entrance to Hong Kong harbor. The onshore wind, blowing against the headland, created a confused sea as the incoming waves met those echoing back from the rocks. At the same time, the funneling effect of the landforms caused a local increase in wind. To save a few minutes and to get some shelter from the headland, I decided to sail in close, although seamanly judgment should have warned me to stand out well past the point before jibing onto the other tack for the first leg into the harbor.

"We'll jibe straight away," I ordered. I could not have made a worse decision. We turned our stern slap into a steep sea that rolled right on over the deck. The main boom had been hauled amidships for the jibe; the torrent of water pouring over the deck entwined the slack mainsheet in the steering gear. I tried to turn the ketch back on course but only succeeded in further jamming the wheel. Rushing on forward, the wave floated the cook-box against a skylight, spilling the spare can of kerosene over the embers of our breakfast fire. Flames leaped up around the mainsail.

"Lower the mainsail!" I cried, hoping that its wet canvas would blanket the fire. But the wave had swirled all the lines around the mainmast into a tangled mess. "Well, cut the damned halyard!" I shouted. We all carried knives in our belts so the halyard was instantly slashed through. But it was the wrong halyard. Down came the jib instead of the main. "No, cut the main halyard!" I bellowed in rising

Wind and Waves

panic. This time someone got the right line and the soaking wet canvas smothered the fire.

But we were still heading for the rocks. My eye fell on the sea anchor we had secured on deck. At least that would act as a brake, I thought, so over the side it went. But nobody watched the line as the anchor drifted away astern; a loop in the rope caught the starting handle of the auxiliary engine and whipped

that overboard, too. Self-starters were then unknown, so there we were—without sails or engine, unable to steer, with a typhoon coming up astern and the waves thumping into some ugly great rocks close ahead. For a moment that seemed eternal, we drifted on toward the crashing surf.

Then the sea anchor took hold. A craft's most self-destructive force is often her own speed, and once she lies stopped in the water, her situation improves dramatically. So it was with us. The moment we realized that we were not, after all, going to be dashed against the rocks, there was a complete change of atmosphere aboard the *Tavy II*. We were all young and resilient, and more frightened than exhausted by our struggles with our own ineptitude. Now, with nothing else to go wrong, we mastered our fears and set about regaining control of our vessel.

One of the crew climbed the mast and rigged a temporary halyard. As my other three friends brought in the sea anchor and hoisted a sail, I took the wheel again. Setting a course well clear of Tathong Point, I eventually brought *Tavy II* into Hong Kong harbor to find that the typhoon had curved away, leaving only rain.

Quick-action Cleats

Many small sailboats carry specialized cleats like the ones right for securing main and jib sheets, which may have to be tied down or released in a hurry. With the jam cleat, one turn and a tug will wedge a line under the cleat's long shoulder. The cam cleat grips a line between two swiveling, serrated cams; simply jerking the line up releases it.

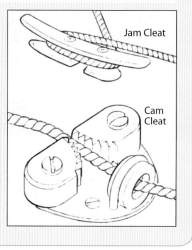

Jam Cleat

Cam Cleat

HINDSIGHT

Always stow or lash down loose gear when it's not in use.

A halyard coil secures the tail of the halyard to the mast cleat after the sail is hoisted. Make a standard coil, pull the innermost loop out through the coil (1) and give the loop several left-hand turns (2). The twisted loop should be long enough to cover the bulk of line making up the coil. With the upper part of the coil laid against the cleat, bring the twisted loop up over the coil and snub it over the top of the cleat (3). When preparing to lower sail, slip the loop off the cleat and drop the coil on deck; the line will run freely.

Another method for binding up a halyard—or any other line—is the sea-gasket coil. After the coil is made up, take three or four feet of line from the back of the coil and make several crosswise turns around the coil (1), starting at the middle and working toward the head. Bring a loop of the working part out through the head of the coil above the turns (2). Slip the loop over the head of the coil and bring it down on top of the turns (3). Pull the working part to draw the loop snug (4). The coil may now be hung up by its working part with assurance that it will not come loose and accidentally unwind.

A stowing coil provides the most reliable way to secure a line that is to be put away in the rope locker. Double the end of the completed coil to form a long loop. Take a clockwise turn around the head of the coil with the loop, passing the end of the loop under its own midsection (1). Take another turn around the coil to the left of the first one (2) and tuck the end of the loop under this second turn. After both turns are pulled tight, the end of the loop stands free (3) and can be hung over a peg. As with all coils, the free end should hang down a short distance so that it does not get lost in the coil.

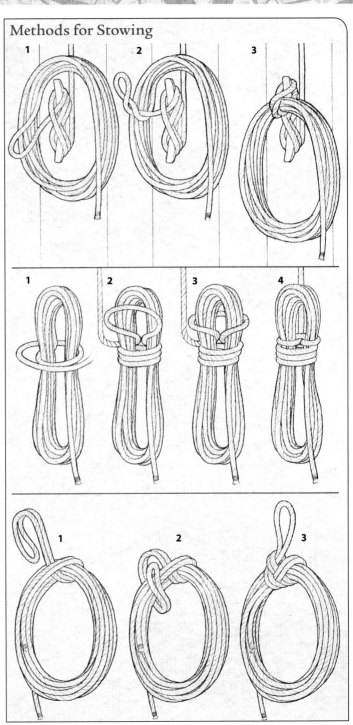

Methods for Stowing

Wind and Waves

Wind and Waves

Wind Patterns

The movement of air from higher to lower pressure areas—the chief cause of the planet's winds—occurs not only on a global scale, but also in tens of thousands of local situations. Although some local winds can be predicted with reasonable accuracy, generally they tend to be more capricious and sometimes stronger than, say, the trade winds that sweep over great stretches of ocean.

Topographical features like mountains, steep headlands or tall trees along a lake shore also can create wind currents, some of them baffling or even dangerous to unwary or inexpert boatmen. A good seaman, however, who has learned how local winds behave, can make them work for him.

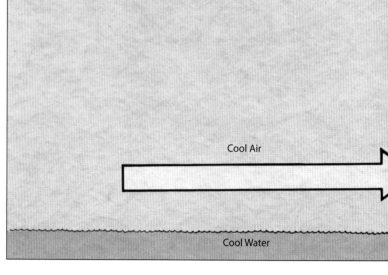

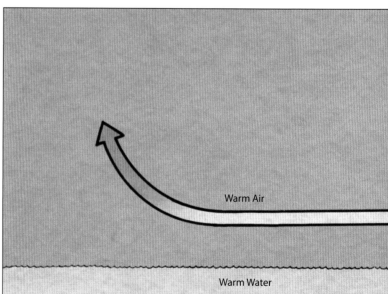

Winds around the Compass

Early mariners gave names to persistent local winds and used them as reference points in navigation. This reproduction of the 15th Century Italian device called a wind rose distinguishes eight major winds, each corresponding in its direction to a cardinal point on the compass. The north wind was the *tramontana*, the wind from the Alps. Moving clockwise around the rose, other symbols denote: *greco* (NE), *levante* (E), *sirocco* (SE), *ostro* (S), *libeccio* (SW), *ponente* (W), and *maestro* (NW).

Among the most common and predictable of local winds are land-sea breeze systems like the one shown above. During the day, land heats up faster than water. Warmed air *(red tint)* rising from the land is replaced by the heavier air of a sea breeze flowing in from over the cooler water surface. At night *(lower diagram)* the land cools more quickly than the sea. Because the heat differential between land and sea is smaller at night, the land breeze tends to be the weaker *(thinner arrow)*.

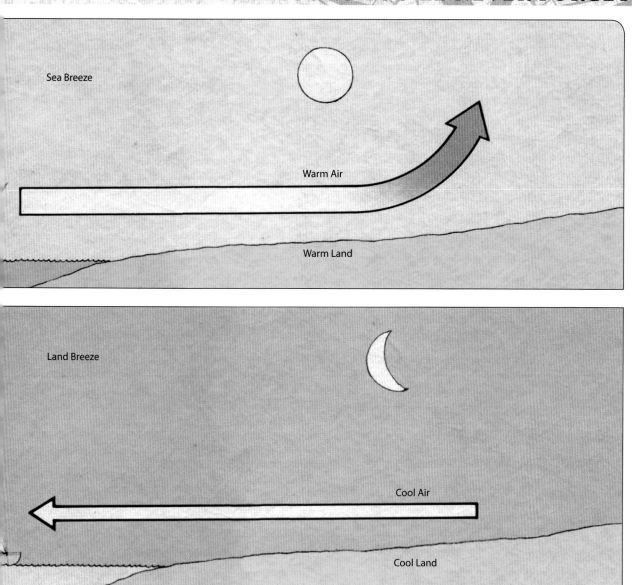

Wind and Waves

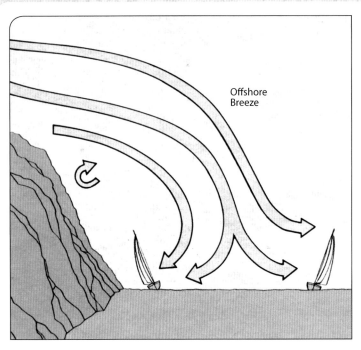

Offshore
Breeze

Offshore winds flowing over a cliff spill out, then down, with some currents curving back toward the escarpment. By the time they have reached the base of the cliff, light breezes can build up, and the boatman should take care not to allow himself to be driven onshore by this reversed wind.

The lower levels of onshore winds are deflected downward by a steep headland, piling up at its base. Where the air descends vertically, there may be no steady wind but only quirky breezes: a sailor close onshore can find himself becalmed one moment, then pushed along by an unexpected gust.

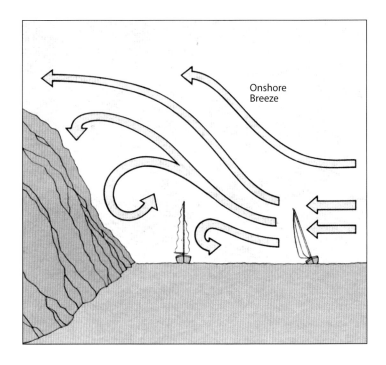

Onshore
Breeze

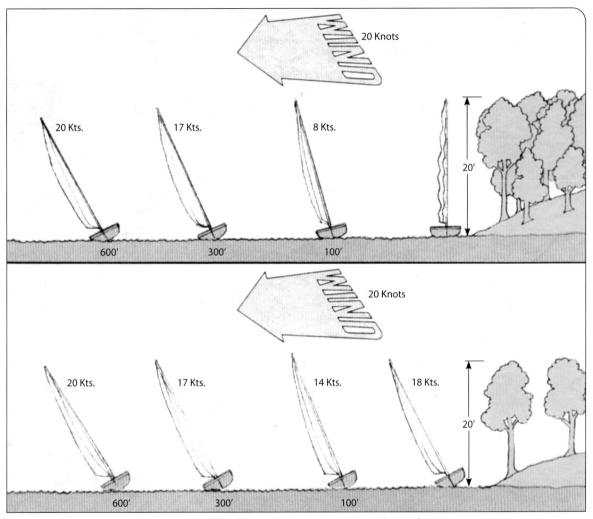

Wind and Waves

A barrier at the water's edge (trees—as here—or houses, or even tall marsh grass) will create an area of reduced and somewhat uneven breeze called a wind shadow, which extends out from shore for a distance of about 30 times the barrier's height. In the lee of a dense barrier *(upper drawing)*, wind speed ranges from zero near shore to full force outside the wind shadow. A less dense barrier produces a fluky effect: the wind blows nearly full force near shore, loses velocity farther out and finally picks up speed again well offshore.

Wind and Waves

Fighting Fires Afloat

Fire at sea is a terrifying and often disastrous experience. If the flames are not quickly extinguished, skipper and crew may have no choice but to abandon ship. Boat fires generally originate from one of three sources: gasoline or diesel fumes, grease or fuel flare-ups from the galley stove, and faulty electric wiring. A careful skipper, therefore, shuts down fuel lines when they are not in use and regularly checks all electrical circuits for loose connections and worn insulation. Furthermore, he installs Coast Guard-approved fire extinguishers at strategic points *(opposite, below)*, and assigns crew members to emergency stations.

The handiest and most effective types of fire extinguishers for boats contain either CO_2 or halon gas, which smother a fire by cutting off its air supply, or dry chemicals that spray a powdery mist over the fire. Both types will snuff out most small fires, though gas works best in enclosed areas where the breeze will not blow it away.

Some boatmen favor foam extinguishers, whose smothering mixture settles solidly on the fire, rather than dissipating or blowing away. But foam is messy to clean up and thus is less practical for minor blazes; and it must never be used on electrical fires, since it may short-circuit exposed wiring. The landsman's favorite extinguisher—water—cannot be entirely relied on at sea, since it is ineffective against gasoline or oil fires. However, very small flare-ups from an alcohol stove can usually be quenched with a cup or two of water from the galley pump.

Firefighter's Check List

If the blaze is from a loose object, such as a deck cushion or ashtray, toss it overboard immediately. If the fire is more serious, the skipper should:

Close down fuel lines or electrical circuits related to or affected by the blaze.

Maneuver the boat so that the wind carries the flames away from the cabin.

Stop all forward motion to avoid fanning the flames.

Localize the fire by closing all adjacent hatches, compartments, and portholes.

Use a fire extinguisher, as shown on the following pages.

Wind and Waves

Fire engulfs a runabout in Vancouver harbor, British Columbia. A spark from the engine set off gasoline fumes that in turn ignited the hull. The fire spread so quickly the skipper had to abandon ship, and the boat burned down to the waterline in a few minutes.

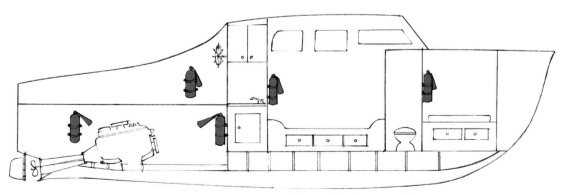

The best locations for fire extinguishers are shown here. At least one extinguisher, and more if space permits, should be permanently mounted on an engine-compartment bulkhead, and operated either by an automatic fire-sensing system or from on deck by remote control *(page 20)*. Another extinguisher, manually operated, should be near the stove. A third should be located at the helm. Auxiliary extinguishers are spotted where they can be reached quickly, near the entry/exit to an enclosed space.

Hazard in the Galley

Most galleys are outfitted with alcohol stoves, which, while inexpensive, are designed in a way that occasionally makes them flare up. Luckily, such fires usually can be put out with a saucepan full of water *(right)*; unlike other liquid fuels, alcohol combines readily with water, thinning out so that it no longer burns. If the fire does not die immediately, however, it should be sprayed with a chemical extinguisher—which Coast Guard regulations require to be on an adjacent bulkhead. Galley curtains should be of fireproof fiberglass, and secured at the hem so that they do not billow over the stove.

This diagram explains why alcohol stoves sometimes flare up. The burner transforms alcohol into a gas by heating it in a vapor chamber. First, the burner control knob is turned on, permitting liquid alcohol to flow into the priming pan. Then, with the knob off, the alcohol is lighted in the pan, starting a small fire that heats the burner—and the vapor chamber. When the knob is turned back on, the incoming alcohol is vaporized in the hot chamber, allowing only gas to escape. If the chamber has not been heated enough by the priming-pan fire, the alcohol remains liquid and flares up when ignited.

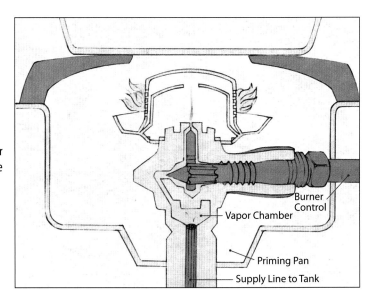

Burner Control

Vapor Chamber

Priming Pan

Supply Line to Tank

Precautions for Storing Stove Gas

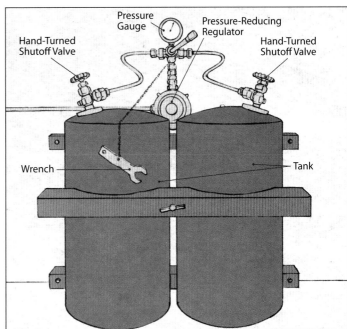

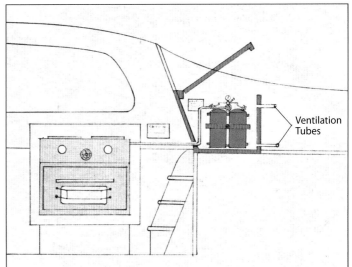

Another popular stove fuel that demands careful handling is tank-stored liquid petroleum gas (LPG), commonly propane or butane. For safety, each LPG tank should have its own hand-controlled shutoff valve, and there should be a pressure-reducing regulator and gauge to monitor gas flow, and a special wrench to fit the tanks' fittings. The tanks must be stored above decks in a well-ventilated compartment with a hatch (lower picture) so that leaking fumes will be carried away. Signs listing precautions and instructions for LPG use should be posted near the tanks and also near the galley stove.

Wind and Waves

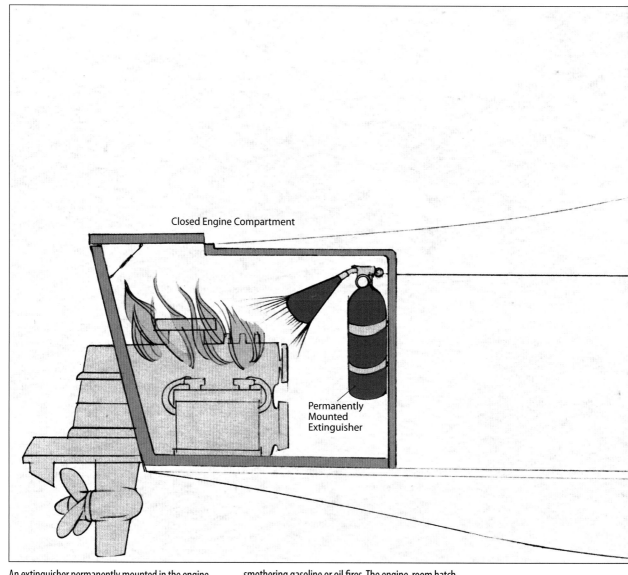

Fuel and Engine Fires

Closed Engine Compartment

Permanently
Mounted
Extinguisher

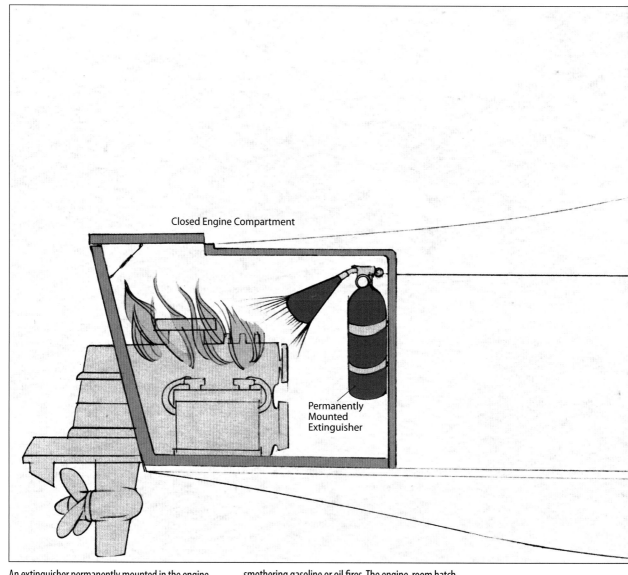

Wind and Waves

An extinguisher permanently mounted in the engine compartment and touched off by remote control, allows a helmsman to quell a blaze without leaving the wheel and losing control of the boat. The extinguisher may be loaded with CO_2, halon gas, or dry chemicals—all suitable for smothering gasoline or oil fires. The engine-room hatch must be kept closed so that no air enters to dissipate the extinguishing agent or feed the flames. Remote systems such as the one shown are so effective that boats equipped with them may qualify for lower insurance rates.

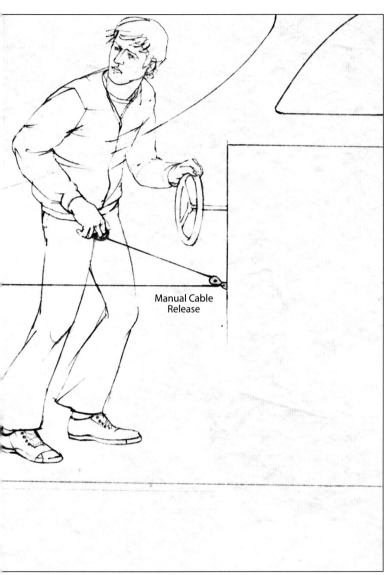

Manual Cable
Release

The Threat of Lightning

Though lightning seldom strikes a boat's hull, it sometimes hits the top of the mast. From there it vents its force within a cone that extends about 60° on either side of the mast and usually includes most of the boat. Within this cone the destructive force is awesome; a wood mast can be snapped off, and the lightning may rip into the boat itself and even set it ablaze. (Metal masts and boats are less hazardous, since they ground lightning automatically.) Ground your wood masts by installing a metal rod at the tip and running a cable to a grounding bolt in the keel. Thus, any part of the boat within the cone escapes damage as the lightning travels along the cable to the keel.

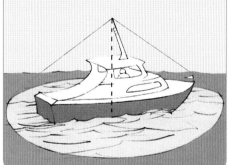

A dry-chemical or gas extinguisher must always be aimed at the base of the fire, where flames can be cut off at their source. To activate the extinguisher, pull the pin in the handle, freeing the trigger. Squeeze the trigger in spurts, sweeping the nozzle back and forth horizontally to arrest the flames.

Foam fire extinguishers should be aimed not directly at the flames but at the overhead or at a bulkhead; the foam then sifts down over the flames, smothering them. With any extinguisher, proper application is vital—the flame-inhibiting blast of common models lasts only 10 to 20 seconds.

A fuel tank and its compartment require ventilation and securing devices to reduce fire hazard. Steel straps lash the tank solidly to the boat's structure, and an interior baffle keeps the fuel from sloshing around. A flexible fuel intake tube gives with the stress motions that occur in any boat. Large vents blow fresh air through the fuel compartment to carry away fumes. A smaller vent inside the tank allows excess fuel to spill harmlessly overboard, carries off fumes and admits air to compensate for changes in fuel levels. Ground wires from the tank to the bonding system render sparks harmless.

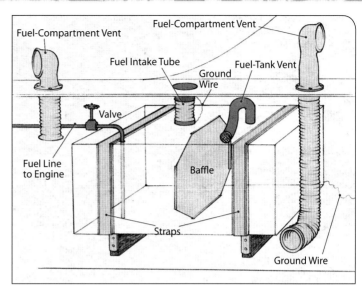

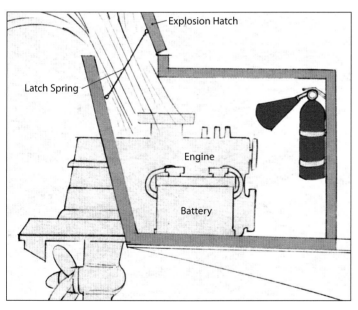

An explosion hatch designed by the Coast Guard directs the force of an engine-compartment blast away from the cabin and crew. If a spark from the engine ignites fuel fumes, or even the hydrogen gas given off by the battery, the blast forces open the explosion hatch. After the explosion, a powerful latch spring pulls the hatch back into place to prevent oxygen in the outside air from feeding the fire that almost immediately follows such explosions. At this point, the skipper must quickly smother the flames with a fire extinguisher.

Wind and Waves

Wind and Waves

Riding Out the Storm

by Erroll Bruce

A big storm in mid-ocean can be a thrilling experience in a thoroughly seaworthy craft whose equipment is intelligently prepared and whose crew can handle it with confidence. Some years ago I was aboard the sloop *Samuel Pepys*, one of three small yachts that set out together from Bermuda bound for Newport, Rhode Island, only to sail unexpectedly into an unseasonal hurricane. In a reversal of my China Sea adventure, the storm really came, but ships and crews were prepared for it; and thus I was able to enjoy— even feel exhilarated at—some of the wilder moments.

The *Samuel Pepys* was only 30 feet long, but she had sturdy lifelines, stout rigging, a full complement of winches and reliable pumps, and her sails were capable of dealing with heavy weather. Furthermore, as the storm built, our precautions were extensive. By the time wind velocity reached about 50 miles an hour, we had lowered all sail and turned to run with the wind—having set several lines, called warps, trailing out at the stern. These were designed to keep us from going so fast, as the screaming wind pressed against the bare rigging, that our nose would bury in a wave.

In addition, the warps helped to break up the crests of following waves and thus keep them from crashing over us. Inside the cabin we had shored up the hatch, the hull's weakest point, with dinghy oars. Anyone in the cockpit was lashed aboard.

After dark the wind struck us with ever more violent gusts as the barometer plummeted. Around midnight the outstanding impression was of noise—the shriek of wind in the rigging and the furious hissing and crashing of the waves breaking around us. In such a situation one cannot fail to be in awe of the wild power of the sea. Yet if you have learned to roll along in time with the violence of the elements, you can actually revel in nature's display of ferocity as great waves mount up and break, while smothers of spray hurtle past you.

After some 15 hours the hurricane had passed over us, and our little vessels, lying to without sails and drifting with the storm, had survived all that turmoil with no damage. Yet a Coast Guard cutter some 10 times our size, on weather patrol in the area, suffered loss of deck equipment by steaming fast through mountainous seas to stand by us.

HINDSIGHT

Always check the weather forecast before heading out on the open water.

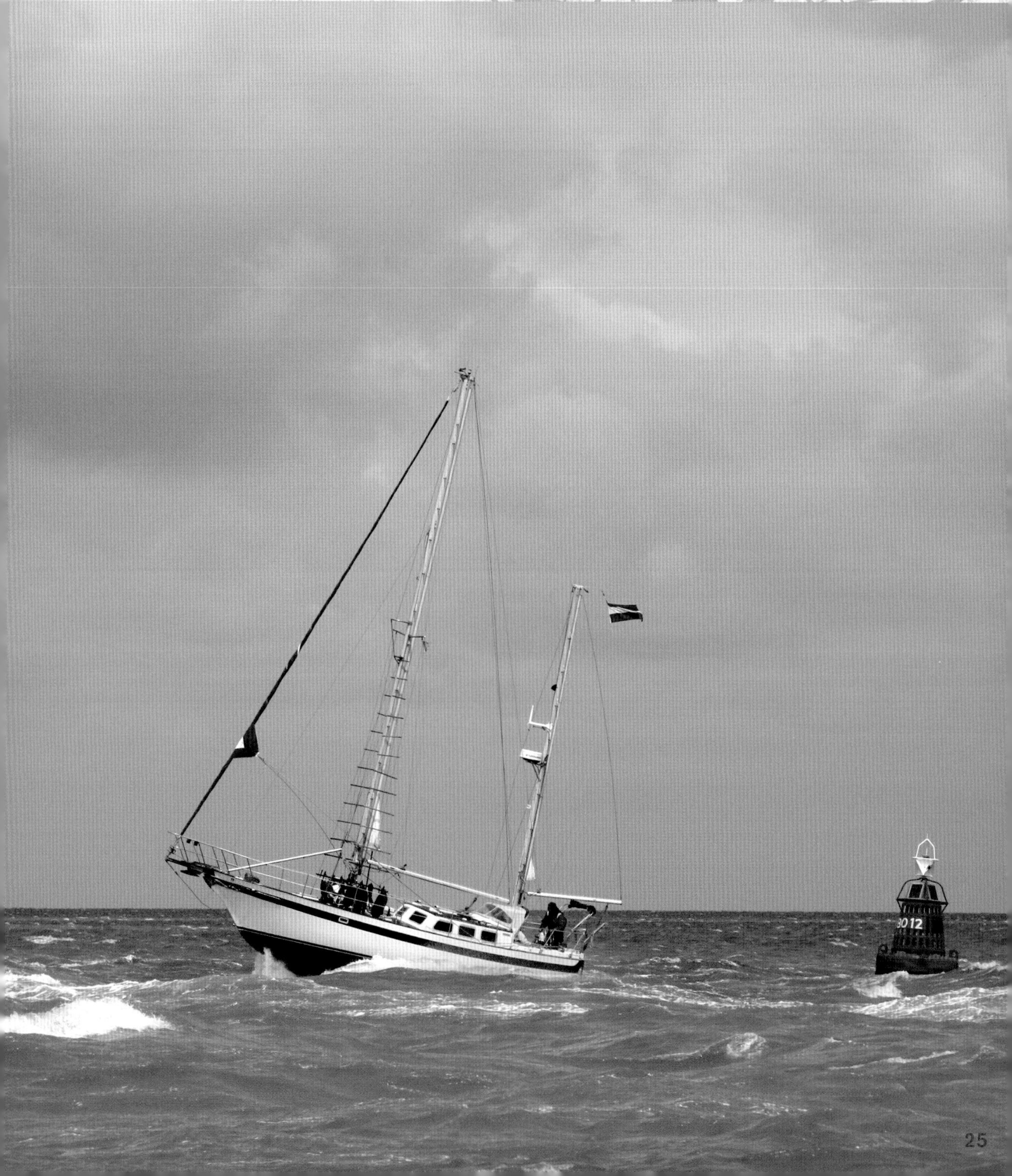

Wind and Waves

Reading the Weather

A boatman is surrounded by an environment composed of powerful and often fickle elements—the skies above, the waters below and the winds around him. As a sound seaman, he must develop a weather eye for the low-lying gray pall of an approaching fog bank, or the swirl of a swift-moving current around a buoy, or the choppy waves that signal shallow water ahead. He is attuned to shifts in the wind and knows how much water the tide has left under his keel. Thus forearmed, he can take full and confident advantage of a favorable current, or slide safely over a shoal at high tide, or run for harbor well ahead of a storm.

Dealing with the elements, like other aspects of good seamanship, requires anticipation based on knowledge—although weather forecasting will always involve a certain amount of guesswork. Before a voyage, ancient Greeks and Romans studied the entrails of sacrificed animals for clues to possible storms. The weather wisdom of other early prophets and seers contained equal parts of empirical knowledge and poetic charm. Saint Matthew advises in the Bible that "when it is evening . . . it will be fair weather, for the sky is red. And in the morning, it will be foul weather today, for the sky is red and lowering." Seamen condensed this observation into a rhyme: "Red sky at morning, sailors take warning. Red sky at night, sailors' delight."

Though hardly infallible, the prophecy holds true to a surprising degree, and has considerable scientific support. The dawn sun gives a rosy hue to low, moisture-bearing clouds that can threaten rain. But a reddish sunset can promise fine sailing because the dust in clear, dry air tends to filter out light of wavelengths other than red.

Sunset off Florida's west coast foreshadows a night of foul boating weather, as a towering thunderstorm advances with a curtain of windy rain hanging from its dark underside.

Wind and Waves

How Weather Works

Much of a mariner's pleasure—and sometimes even his life—depends on how well he reads the moods of the weather immediately around him. However, the localized weather on any given body of water is always linked to larger weather patterns; and a grasp of those larger patterns is essential in helping the seaman understand what is happening at the moment and what may be coming up next.

The fundamental fact of a U.S. weather watcher's life is that most weather tends to come from a westerly direction. Boatmen on the lakes of Missouri keep an eye on conditions in Arizona and New Mexico to learn what is headed their way; the rain that Lake Michigan sailors had yesterday, Chesapeake Bay sailors probably will have tomorrow. This is because for most of Canada and the lower 48 states, except for parts of Florida and Texas, the prevailing winds are westerlies, as illustrated in the map of global air circulation on page 30. Under the more or less constant urging of these immense atmospheric currents, the storms and rainy spells that interrupt the boating season move in succession from west to east across the land.

How fast they move, however, and just what they will do is not so easy to forecast. In some parts of the world to be sure—where the trade winds blow, for instance—conditions are so stable that the same patterns recur day after day. But North America's temperate zone is overlaid by a mosaic of hot and cold air masses *(below, left)* that are in continual conflict. The area where the leading edge of one air mass bumps into another is known as a front, and along that battle line the weather is in constant turmoil.

The essential cause of this turbulence is temperature difference. Cold air is dense, and therefore heavy, and it tends to hug the ground. Warm air is lighter and when confronted by cold air generally rises, cools and condenses. This interplay almost always produces clouds and usually rain. It may also result in violent storms.

Basically there are four kinds of fronts and each produces its own kind of weather, as shown in the schematic drawings at right. The boatman who learns how to recognize the kind of front he has encountered is likely to know what kind of weather he should prepare for.

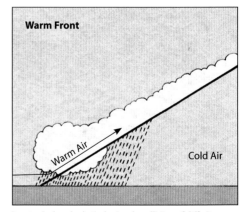

Warm Front

Warm Air

Cold Air

In a typical and relatively simple collision of differing atmospheric conditions, the leading edge of a mass of warm air moves with characteristic slowness as it overtakes the trailing edge of a cold air mass. Moisture in the rising air cools and condenses into precipitation. Until the front passes—and for a few days thereafter— boatmen in the area can expect foggy, soggy weather.

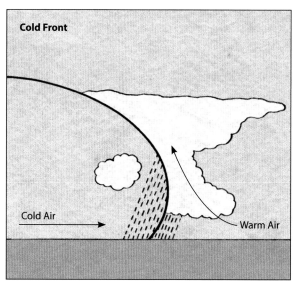

An incoming cold front travels faster and has a more violent impact than does a warm front. The relatively cold and heavy air pushes up the warmer air in front of it, forcing the warm air to release its moisture as precipitation—often accompanied by wind squalls and lightning. This stormy interlude may be rough on the boatman, but after the front passes he can be assured of some days of clear, cooler weather.

A more complex weather change, called a cold-front occlusion, takes place when a cold front overtakes and drives upward a warm air mass—and then presses on and bumps into still another air mass that is cool, but less cold than the overtaking mass. The latter encounter is usually marked by light, steady rains from the warm front, followed by the strong winds and the colder temperatures normally associated with a cold front.

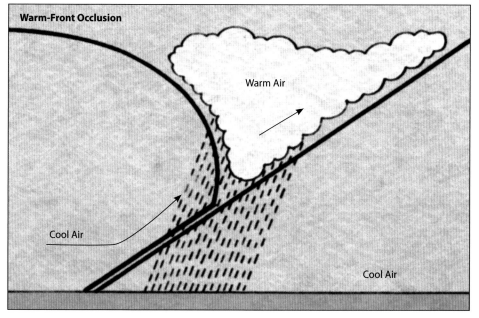

When a cold front pushes aside a body of intervening warm air and overtakes an even colder air mass, the result is called—paradoxically—a warm-front occlusion. The intervening warm mass is forced upward and so is the advancing cold front as it encounters the even colder air. The resulting activity, less severe than that of a cold-front occlusion, yields precipitation, followed by warmer temperatures.

Wind and Waves

29

Wind and Waves

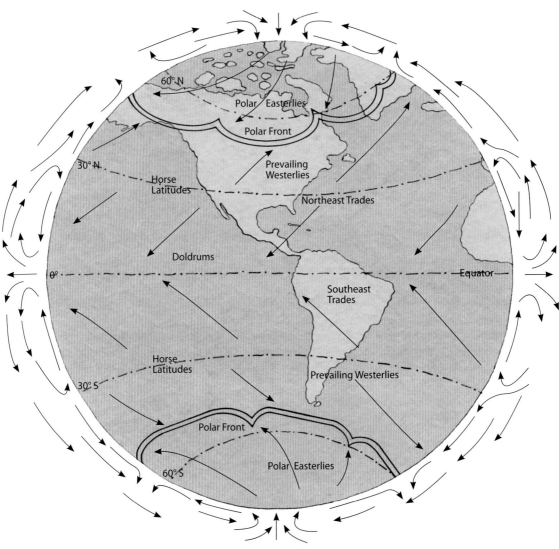

The westerly winds that keep weather moving eastward across the United States are part of the orderly pattern of global winds illustrated above. Hot air rising from the equator flows toward the poles, periodically cools, sinks, and eventually moves back toward the equator. The contrary movement of these air flows results in bands of calms like those of the doldrums and the so-called horse latitudes; combined with the effects of the earth's rotation, they create bands of steady winds such as the polar easterlies, the easterly trades, and the prevailing westerlies.

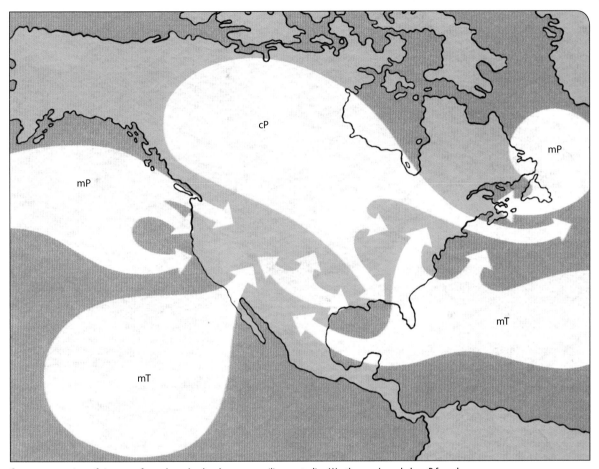

Constant processions of air masses formed over land and sea cross the boundaries of North America from north, south, and west, and then move east under the impetus of the prevailing westerlies. Weathermen's symbols—P for polar, T for tropical, m for maritime and c for continental—mark the regions in which each kind of air mass originated.

Wind and Waves

Stratus clouds occur in a solid or mottled layer, and rarely portend good weather. At ground level they become fog. A little higher, they usually bring a light drizzle—and often may hide approaching thunderheads.

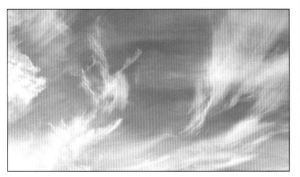

Cirrus clouds always appear at high levels, and if moving in from the northwest, they usually indicate a fine day. But if a series of lower, thickening clouds follow the cirrus clouds, rain or snow is probably imminent.

Cirrocumulus clouds, sometimes arranged in patterns like the scales of a mackerel, indicate changeable weather—as recognized in an ancient couplet: "Mackerel sky, mackerel sky/ Not long wet, not long dry."

In the temperate zone across the United States, clouds occur at altitudes up to 45,000 feet—above which low temperatures prevent cloud formation. Anywhere between 16,500 and 45,000 feet are cirrus, cirrocumulus and cirrostratus. Altocumulus, altostratus and nimbostratus are usually found from 6,500 to 23,000 feet, although the latter two may build a bit higher or lower. Stratocumulus and stratus form only beneath 6,500 feet, and the latter may descend to ground level. Cumulus and cumulonimbus have bases starting below 6,500 feet; but a cumulonimbus can raise its menacing head up to 45,000 feet.

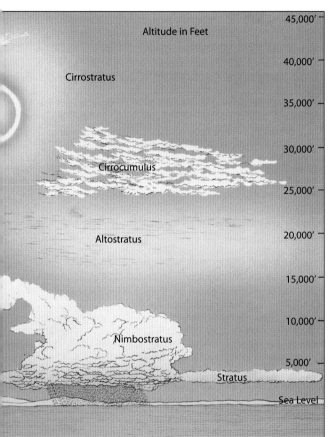

Altitude in Feet

45,000'

40,000'

Cirrostratus

35,000'

30,000'

Cirrocumulus

25,000'

Altostratus

20,000'

15,000'

10,000'

Nimbostratus

5,000'

Stratus

Sea Level

Signs in the Sky

Though complex when used by meteorologists, cloud language can be remarkably clear to laymen. Low clouds, for instance, are the most likely to yield unwanted gifts like rain or snow. Generally, the blacker and sharper the edge of an advancing thundercloud, the more forbidding its portent.

Though clouds may look stable at first glance they are almost constantly, and often rapidly, changing. The changes can be as meaningful as the original or ultimate shapes. Mutating clouds often warn a boatman of a fast-rising local storm before his radio can. Weather broadcasts are normally updated every three to six hours; cumulus clouds mounting vertically and darkening at the lower edges as they change to cumulonimbus can bring violent rain and wind within 90 minutes.

Snow-white puffs of cumulus against a deep blue sky are a universal fair-weather sign. If they suddenly should darken and begin to build to towering heights, however, they warn of violent thunderstorms brewing.

Cirrostratus is a high-altitude rain-or snow-warning cloud that can overcast the entire sky. It causes the halos around the sun or the moon—which, for good reason, are linked in folklore with the coming of bad weather.

A seagoing tornado, or waterspout, is made up of spray and moisture from the air, shaped into a column by the cyclonic winds in a thunderstorm or a squall line. It can produce winds of up to 130 knots, and the extreme low pressure at its center can explode a small vessel caught in its erratic path.

An advancing squall line, such as this one, poses one of the most dangerous threats to a seaman. Actually a chain of thunderstorms that can stretch out as far as 500 miles, a squall line advances ahead of a cold front and brings with it winds of up to 100 knots. Commonly, a squall line will travel at a rate of about 30 knots; but a more powerful one, moving as fast as 50 knots, can easily overtake almost any small vessel within an hour after first being sighted and can then last up to 20 hours.

The classic sign of a thunderstorm, and a clear warning to all boatmen in the vicinity, is the swiftly rising thunderhead. A thunderhead can form within an hour, and the one at left, probably not much older than that, is already releasing a downpour. This storm will soon exhaust itself, but the conditions that bred it may spawn others.

Stormy Weather

Every sensible seaman prefers to avoid squalls—by which a sailor means the sudden, strong winds that accompany anything from a lone thunderstorm *(far left at bottom)* to a marching line of ministorms *(left)*. Such ultimate terrors as waterspouts *(far left at top)* are too unpredictable for realistic concern; and the hurricanes that lash the Atlantic and Gulf coasts in summer and fall are almost always spotted far enough in advance to let boatmen batten down in a secure harbor well before the storm hits.

But thunderstorms, however brief, are a menace to mariners with their high winds, rain, lightning, dangerously choppy seas and occasional hail. On humid summer afternoons or whenever a cold front is reported in his area, a boatman should watch for towering cumulonimbus clouds. Cold air falling down from the peaks of the tall clouds gathers speed as it rushes toward the surface. It arrives as violent and frequent gusts of great force that change direction rapidly and unpredictably. A boatman in the path of an advancing thundercloud may not be able to get back to port before the storm strikes. But he almost always has time to put on foul weather clothes, lower his sails and close the hatches before being engulfed.

Wind and Waves

Profile of a Storm System

A typical storm system, diagramed here, consists of a warm front followed in a day or two by a cold front—with a low-pressure center where the fronts join. To orient himself in respect to the system, a boatman should face the wind. The low-pressure center will always be on his right. If the barometer is falling and the wind is shifting counterclockwise, the storm center will miss the boatman at point A above. At B, however, the wind is shifting clockwise as the barometer falls, and the boatman there will be in the storm system's path.

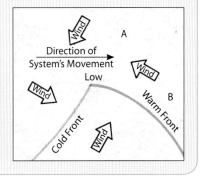

Wind and Waves

Fear Was Our Constant Companion

by Erroll Bruce

The most diabolical seas I myself have ever seen were not those in mid-ocean but in a channel only seven miles wide—the Pentland Firth, which separates the Orkney Islands from the mainland of Scotland. Storms have lashed this channel to such fury that once, early in this century, a great British battleship had her bridge carried away. Simply to take a boat out into such waters in stormy weather and bring her safely back demands seamanship of the highest order. Yet into that very channel, no matter what the weather, must venture the volunteer crews of the Royal National Lifeboat Institute, in daylight or dark, responding to calls from vessels in distress.

I was for a time one of eight volunteers in a 40-foot motor lifeboat based at the tiny hamlet of Long Hope in the Orkneys. On many a wild winter's night we were among the boats called out to duty. Each of us rushed from his warm bed to the lifeboat station, and while the launchers prepared the boat, we donned oilskins and life belts, quickly but carefully. The coxswain always insisted that each of us check the adjustments of the next man's life belt and even delayed launching a minute if one man's strap was twisted. Then at his signal the boat began her skid down the steep runway.

The sea usually greeted her with a wave that raked her from bow to stern. Engines full ahead, wheel hard over, she would swing round at the touch of the coxswain, who stood upright, strapped to his tubular steel backrest. The rest of us sat grimly clinging to various parts of the pitching, rolling, plunging boat. There was no

> ## HINDSIGHT
> Fear of the unknown can interfere with coolheaded judgment.

chance then to adjust a life belt; anyone who let go with even one hand as the boat rode those monstrous seas risked being flung overboard. The darkness was a devil-black obscurity that shocked the mind as spray-laden gusts bit into our cheeks. And after completing our mission we had still to make the equally perilous journey home. Every trip was a flawless exhibition of thorough preparation and expert execution.

Fear was our constant companion on those dark winter nights with the gale hurling snow, hail, and spray into our faces as we searched anxiously among the waves for those in distress. Yet our fear was reasoned and controlled; it was not an enemy—as when I panicked off Hong Kong—but our friend, sharpening our senses, heightening our awareness of danger and prompting us to meet it with the quick but measured actions of true seamen.

The time to establish this prudence, these sure reflexes, is before emergencies arise. A calm day with plenty of sea room for correcting a mistake or two is a good occasion for practicing the use of, say, an oar jury-rigged as emergency steering gear aboard your powerboat—or, on a sailboat, for setting a storm trysail or simply reefing the main. The good seaman should never wait for emergencies to practice such skills.

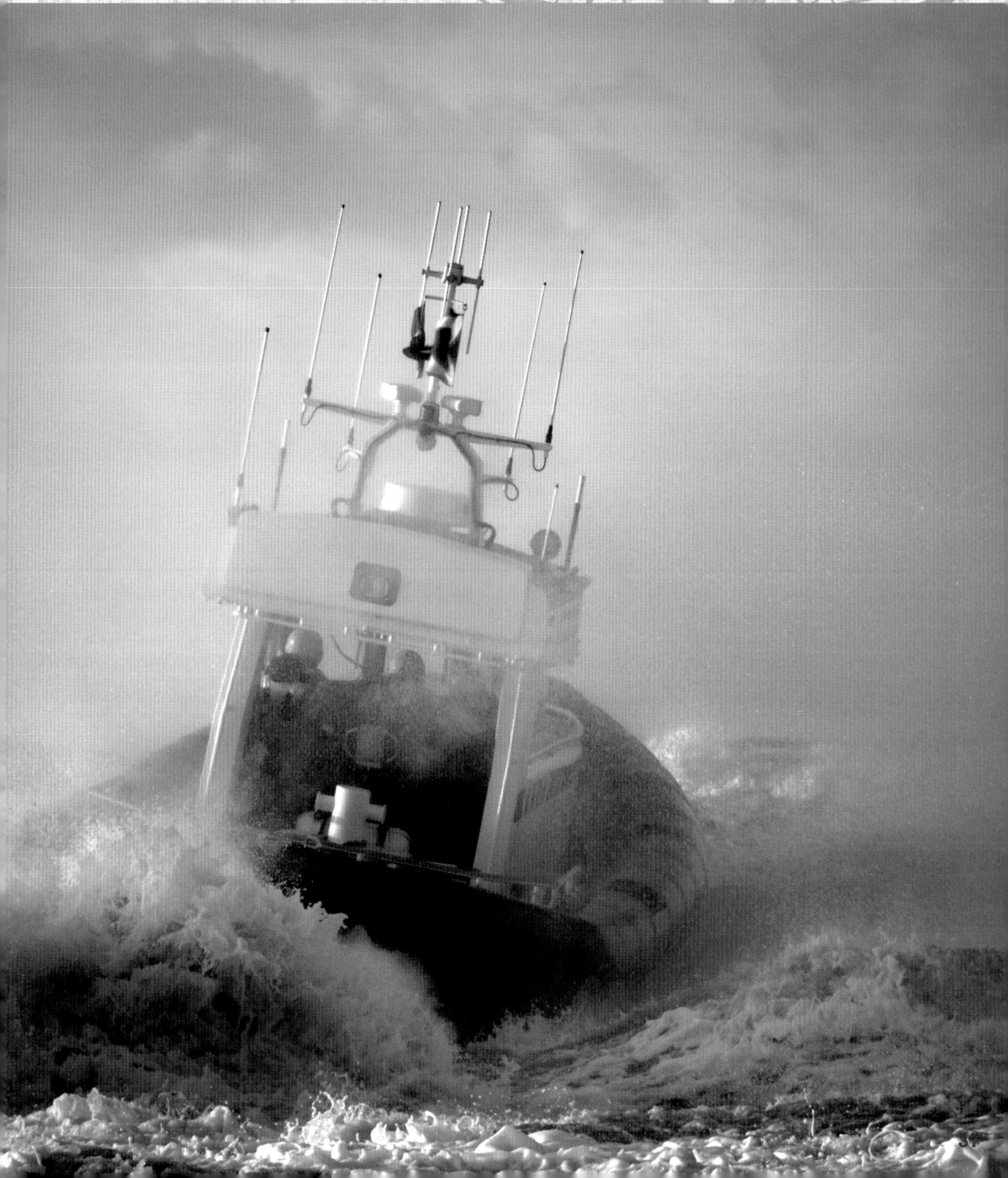

Wind and Waves

Man Overboard

On the stormy sixth day of the 1960 Bermuda Race, the yawl *Scylla*, under a small jib, heavily reefed main and mizzen, drove south through the Gulf Stream against 50-knot head winds and 35-foot waves. At about midnight, crewman Jack Weston came off watch and, unhooking his safety harness from the railing, started down the companionway. At that moment, the boat swung violently into the trough of a wave. As the vessel lurched, Weston popped out of the hatch like a champagne cork. Sea water washing heavily over the deck swept him under the port life line and into the sea.

Despite the pitch black of mid-ocean storm conditions, another crewman, who was tending the mizzen, saw Weston go. Crying "Man overboard!", the mizzenhand heaved over a life ring with a rescue light attached to it. At the same time, the helmsman checked *Scylla's* heading on the compass and called it out to the navigator, who noted it down. If Weston was to be found as quickly as possible, the boat would have to be put into a 180° turn and sailed back along a reciprocal course. To prepare for the turn, the crew began taking down sail and got ready to start up the engine.

With the sails already struck, the engine failed to start. The battery was dead; but forethought saved the situation. Before sailing, Weston himself had made *Scylla* a present of a 12-volt spare battery and a pair of jump cables. They were instantly hooked up, and the engine rumbled to life.

Weston, meanwhile, flailed about miserably in *Scylla's* wake. "I had no hope they could get

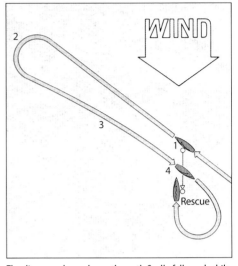

The diagram above shows the path Scylla followed while rescuing Weston. After Weston was catapulted into the sea (1), the crew struck the sails and started the diesel to jibe the boat around. But heavy seas lifted the propeller out of water so often that the jib had to be raised to assist with the turn (2). Taking a return course (3) that allowed for Weston's being swept to leeward, Scylla approached downwind on a port tack, so that the crew could haul him aboard on the lee side (4). But the wind carried the boat by too fast for a pickup. Scylla had to jibe again and headed into the wind; Weston was lifted aboard by a swell after almost an hour in the water.

back to me," he said later. "I wondered how long it would take to drown, and what it would feel like." Then he caught sight of the strobe light, flashing perhaps a hundred yards away. Unable to swim for it along the surface of the cresting seas, he set off in a series of underwater dives.

When he reached the light, Weston began treading water and waving the strobe overhead. Finally the boat hove into sight, and Weston was grappled aboard by two crewmen—exhausted and still thoroughly frightened, but safe.

Wind and Waves

Flung overboard by a wave during the Bermuda Race, Jack Weston brandishes a flashing strobe light to guide his rescuers to him. After he swam to the light, he failed to realize, in the dark and confusion, that it was attached to a life ring, and he treaded water until he was picked up. Strobe lights of this type, which are visible for a distance of many miles under normal conditions, have since been declared mandatory equipment for all boats on Bermuda Races.

REMINDER

Always assign one person to keep a constant eye on the crew in the water.

Wind and Waves

Search and Pickup

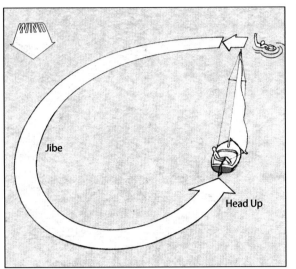

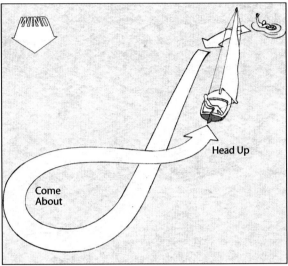

The fastest way to retrieve a man who has fallen overboard is to jibe, then circle back into the wind and bring the boat to a stop to weather of the man. The helmsman or crew can then proffer a hand, a line, or a boathook.

In heavy weather, the best pickup plan is to bear off briefly, then come about to cross the former course before heading up just to weather of the swimmer. The hull will shield the man in the water from wave action.

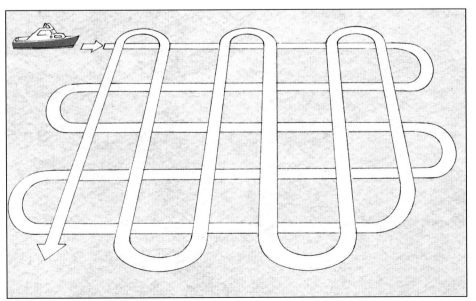

At night, in fog or in choppy seas, a man overboard may drift quietly out of sight. In such cases, the skipper should instantly lay a course toward the man's last position, then begin crisscrossing the area in a pattern like that shown above, with a lookout posted as high up on the vessel as possible. By sticking to this method, one skipper in a transpacific race rescued a man lost overboard 20 hours earlier.

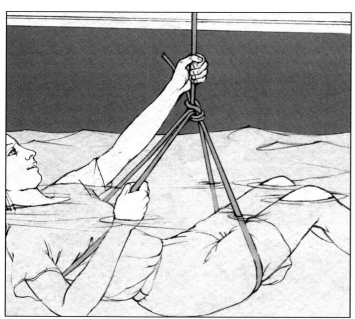

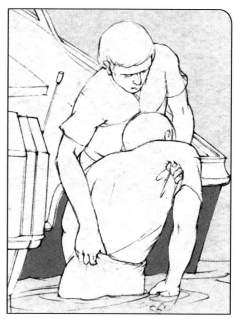

When a person overboard is too weak or heavy to be hauled in by hand, a bowline on a bight secured to the mainsheet, makes a good rig for helping the rescued one aboard. Rescuers begin by heaving a line with a loop in the end that the person can grab to be drawn to the ship's side. Then the swimmer wriggles into the bowline's double loops. The crew stays aboard unless the person rescued is unconscious or in imminent danger of drowning. A shipmate who leaps into the water to help doubles the number of people to be rescued and reduces the number of effective crew members aboard.

A person overboard reentering a small boat, whether clambering in by himself or being hauled aboard as here, should make his entry over the stern. Any attempt to get aboard amidships or over the bow can end in a capsize, and in rough water a plunging bow may knock a swimmer unconscious.

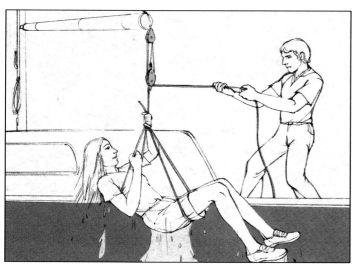

With the rescued person well balanced in a bowline on a bight tied to the lower block of the mainsheet purchase, a crewman hauls his shipmate back aboard. If possible, another crewman should steady the boom. The person overboard can aid importantly in his own rescue by staying calm, shedding heavy clothing and floating quietly rather than exhausting himself by frantic—and futile—swimming.

CHAPTER 2:
Animal Encounters

Animal encounters, whether watching dolphins play in your wake or seeing a whale breach off the starboard side, can be one of the most charming aspects to being out on the water. On rare occasions, animal encounters such as the ones in the following pages can be the most dangerous. With no notice, these boaters survived by knowing what to do when disaster struck. A boater's best protection is to remember that these are wild animals despite how charming they may be. Most wild animals are shy and would rather avoid humans. The 40-ton whale that crashed down on a sailboat off the coast of South Africa may have been just due to poor eyesight and being in the wrong place at the wrong time. However, other boaters in the area have suggested that the whale was being harassed prior to the incident. Keeping an appropriate distance would be the first step in avoiding animal encounters.

Whale watching such as the tourists in this dinghy are doing is much more comfortable from a distance.

Animal Encounters

Attacked by a Great White

In December the southern Indian Ocean is normally blessed with sparkling days, ample breezes and few cares for the sailor. It was on just such a morning, on December 15, 1971, that William King, an experienced skipper in his mid-sixties, was heading west off the tip of Australia on his way to Cape Horn—"alone with my lovely boat in the ocean," he later wrote. Suddenly a horrifying impact rocked the boat, opening a splintered three-foot wound in its hull. Rushing on deck from the cabin King saw a green swirl astern—the trail of a huge shark that had just rammed him.

King's boat, the 42-foot *Galway Blazer II*, had been custom designed and fitted out to meet almost any challenge the sea might offer. Junk-rigged for easy handling, her cigar-shaped, laminated plywood hull was built to withstand any amount of battering by the sea—but not a chance-in-a-million shark attack.

The hull was stove in underwater on the lee side, but by some quick and deft seamanship *(right)* King managed to turn his boat so that the hole rose above the surface. Next he began the enormous task of bailing out the ton or so of water the boat had shipped before he changed tacks. Lacking an electric bilge pump, he had to hand-pump every 10 to 15 minutes for the next four days, breaking only to eat, catnap and perform major patchwork on the hull, both inside and out. Fortunately, the plywood at the point of impact had not completely ruptured; however, its glued laminations had sprung apart and it had many small rents.

By the fourth day most of the water had been pumped from the hull, and King could concentrate on adding more bracing and caulking to improve his repair. Five days later he felt confident enough to put the damaged area below water and turn back to Fremantle, Australia, 600 miles away. As he entered the harbor on December 30, after having ridden out 40-knot winds en route, a kindly Australian voice called out to him from the dock: "You look cut up. How about a nice strong cup of tea?"

HINDSIGHT

Believing that red antifouling paint had appeared to the shark as blood and had provoked the attack, King later painted the craft's underside green.

Holed by a huge white shark in the Indian Ocean, the junk-rigged yacht Galway Blazer II sails close-hauled on port tack. Only by heeling the boat well over and holding to this tack could skipper William King keep the damaged area above water. But the course took him ever farther out to sea. He was 400 miles from Australia when the incident occurred; by the time he had patched the hull and could turn back, he had gone another 200 miles.

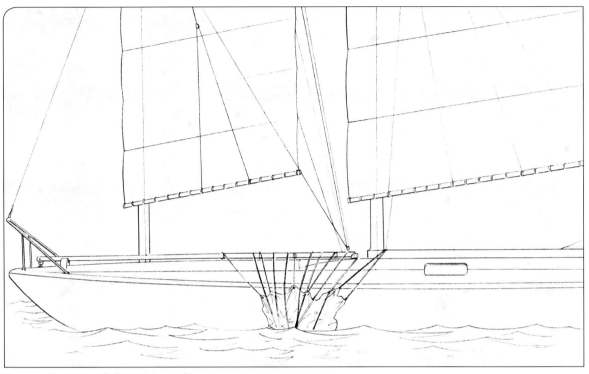

Exterior patching consisted of multiple layers of foam
rubber, sailcloth, a hatch cover, and even King's waterproof
rubber trousers, all bound securely by 13 separate lines
wrapped around the hull and tied down like the ribbons
on a Christmas package.

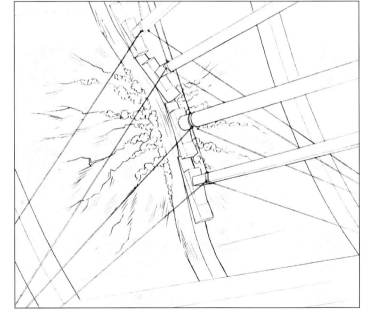

Internal bracing shored up a vertical rib that lay across
the center of the damaged area and held it together.
Although the rib was sprung inward, King managed to
keep it from breaking by wedging a spare boom, sawed
down to the width of the cabin, from the rib's center to a
structural member on the cabin's opposite side.

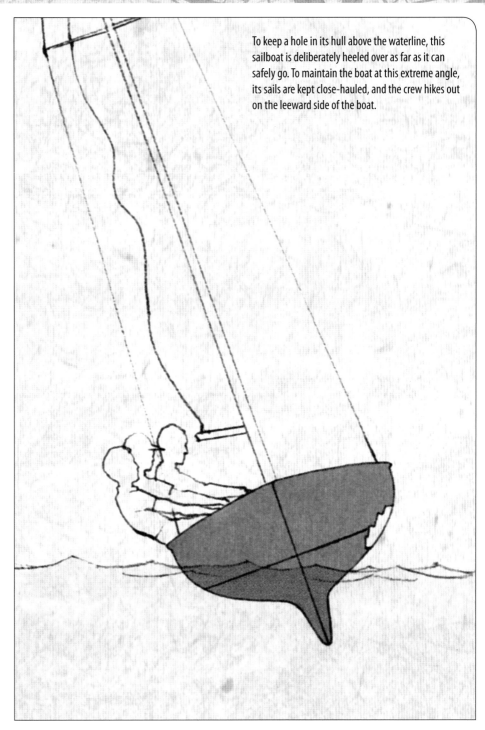

To keep a hole in its hull above the waterline, this sailboat is deliberately heeled over as far as it can safely go. To maintain the boat at this extreme angle, its sails are kept close-hauled, and the crew hikes out on the leeward side of the boat.

Animal Encounters

47

How To Bail Unwanted Water

Once a boat has taken on unwanted water, the skipper should bail it out as soon as possible, using one of the types of bilge pumps shown here. Many inboard-powered boats have an electric pump in the engine compartment or a hand pump permanently mounted near the helm. A portable hand pump should also be carried for emergency duty anywhere on the boat. And as extra insurance in the event of pump failure, every skipper should learn how to jury-rig an engine's cooling system to move water from the bilges *(below)*.

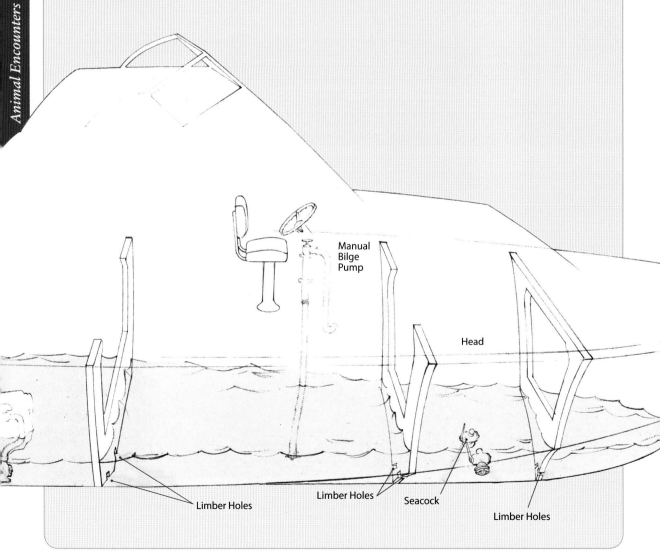

Manual Bilge Pump

Head

Limber Holes

Limber Holes

Seacock

Limber Holes

Every boat's stock of emergency equipment should include such crucial spare parts as those shown here. They include: an auxiliary tiller *(top left, next to oar)*, fan belts, as well as wire rope and U-bolts (under the rope coils). Small, easily lost items—fuses, spark plugs, electrical wire, cotter pins, shear pins, and turnbuckles—can be stowed in a box *(center, left)*. In addition, the boatowner is wise to keep scrap wood, corks, stout twine, and a tarpaulin *(bottom)* for making repairs.

In open water during daytime, dye marker stains the water yellow-green or orange to attract passing aircraft that can then radio for help. The dye usually comes as a powder; but do not simply shake it overboard, as the wind may scatter it. Instead, dissolve it in a can of seawater and empty the bucket slowly at water level. The stain, visible for 10 miles from the air, lasts 30 minutes in a calm sea.

Signaling for Help

When trouble strikes at sea, a boat's captain should have two instantaneous responses: (1) go after the problem—or order someone else to do so; (2) call for help. And *never* hesitate to call for help. The Coast Guard would much rather arrive early to find all well than show up too late to help.

Basically, any means of signaling that attracts attention is a good one. Use radio if you have it. Of any visual signals, the ones shown here have proved most effective. Each makes use of brilliant, eyecatching colors. The sudden glare of a red flare at night generates quick attention, and in daylight the vibrant stain of dye marker, the cloud of a smoke bomb, or bright flashes of waving cloth will usually bring help in a short time.

Any boat that does not have radio should be equipped to give at least one daytime and one nighttime visual distress signal. But even on boats with electronic devices *(pages 51–53)*, there ought to be some visual signaling equipment aboard in case power fails or the radio transmitter breaks down.

Radio Distress Calls

The best way to get help in an emergency at sea is to broadcast a distress signal by radio. The Coast Guard and many civilian boats and planes constantly monitor radio distress frequencies. Sets range in sophistication and price from a compact emergency beacon *(lower right)*, which costs about the same as an inexpensive TV set, to elaborate satellite phone installations costing as much as a car. Any boatman can match his investment to his budget and cruising habits; and it is a needless risk to venture beyond sight of land without radio equipment.

Although using a radiotelephone may seem complicated to the novice, these instruments are simple to operate. Every boatman owning a set should know how to send and receive distress calls before he leaves the dock so that his response to an emergency *(box, page 53)* will be immediate and confident.

If a genuine crisis should occur—sinking, fire or acute illness—the boatman should send what is known as a "mayday" call (derived from *m'aider*, French for "help me"): the first word spoken is may-day. Mayday calls have first priority; and all other radio transmission stops when a mayday is heard. However, if life is not in immediate danger but help is needed—if you are out of gas, lost or run aground—send a "pan" call (from *panne*, French for "breakdown"). Pan calls have second priority. Important weather, navigation and other marine safety information is preceded by the word "security."

Federal regulations require all new marine radio stations to use VHF-FM sets. But VHF-FM reception, though clear and reliable, is limited to a 20-mile range. Thus boats cruising farther offshore ought to carry an emergency beacon, which has a much longer range.

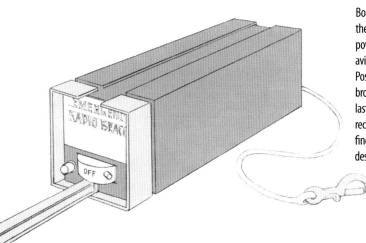

Boats without radiotelephone and those that cruise beyond the 20-mile range of shore stations should carry a battery-powered transmitter that broadcasts a distress signal over aviation emergency channels. Officially called an Emergency Position Indicating Radio Beacon, the nine-inch transmitter broadcasts continually for eight days (in storage, the batteries last up to 19 months), beaming a tone signal audible on receivers up to 200 miles away. Rescue craft with direction finders can home in on the signal even when the transmitter, designed to be buoyant, is afloat in its waterproof case.

Many GPS units now come with a transceiver built in to send messages in case of an emergency.

DATE	TIME	STATION CALLED / RECEIVED	CALL LETTERS	LOG MES
8/3/75	0815	Rec'd Sea Sprite	KL7074	May da 110° Ca
"	0817	Called "	"	Acknou May da
"	0825	Rec'd. "	"	Immee requeste
"	0827	Called "	"	Under w ETA 08
"	0835	Rec'd. "	"	C G picl Sea Spr

Keep a log book and at least two durable pens (in emergencies, pencils tend to break and single pens to go dry) by the transceiver, and immediately record incoming distress messages and your response, as shown here. This information must be available as the emergency develops, and cannot be trusted to memory, especially in times of stress.

Radio Distress Calls

When life is in danger, begin a distress call with the word mayday repeated three times. Then transmit your radio call sign (i.e., station number) three times and your boat name three times. Follow with a full distress message, beginning again with "mayday" and next giving your call sign, boat name, location, conditions aboard and the identifying characteristics of your boat. For example: "Mayday. Mayday. Mayday. This is KL 7074. KL 7074. KL 7074. Sea Sprite. Sea Sprite. Sea Sprite." After a short pause, continue: "Mayday. KL 7074. Sea Sprite. Bearing one hundred and ten degrees true off Catalina Island. Distance about three miles. Fire out of control. Four persons aboard. May have to abandon ship. Vessel is thirty-foot cabin cruiser, black hull, white trim. Over." Then stand by for replies.

In a lesser emergency, when you need help but life is not in immediate danger, send a message patterned after the one given above, but use the word pan instead of mayday.

The phonetic spelling alphabet is often the best means for spelling out radio call signs and any other words that may not be clearly understood. In the message above, the call sign could be spoken Kilo Lima 7074—and should be given this way if a repeat is requested.

A Alfa	**H** Hotel	**O** Oscar	**V** Victor
B Bravo	**I** India	**P** Papa	**W** Whiskey
C Charlie	**J** Juliett	**Q** Quebec	**X** X-ray
D Delta	**K** Kilo	**R** Romeo	**Y** Yankee
E Echo	**L** Lima	**S** Sierra	**Z** Zulu
F Foxtrot	**M** Mike	**T** Tango	
G Golf	**N** November	**U** Uniform	

If you hear a distress message like the one given above, immediately stop any broadcast you may be sending. Listen to see if the message is answered. If it is not, then answer, giving the distressed vessel's call sign and name first and then your own. Follow this sequence: "KL [or Kilo Lima] 7074. KL 7074. KL 7074. Sea Sprite. Sea Sprite. Sea Sprite. This is WD [or Whiskey Delta] 4126. WD 4126. WD 4126. Mary Jane. Received mayday. Over." Pause momentarily for other stations to acknowledge the mayday call. Then contact the vessel in distress and offer assistance. Determine from subsequent transmissions between you, the distressed vessel and any other vessels that may answer, who is in the best position to help. If you are closest, let the distressed vessel know that you are proceeding to its aid and at what time you will probably arrive. Keep it informed of your progress. If you do not go to help, stand by on the emergency channel until you are certain that someone has reached the stricken boat and that you are no longer needed.

Animal Encounters

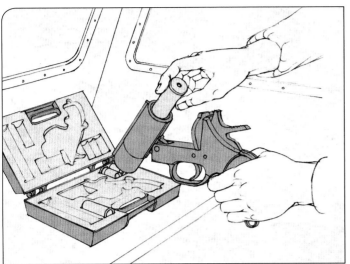

The most effective night signal is a flare, launched from a so-called Very pistol *(left)*. Even by day these red flares can be used to summon rescuers. Load the pistol by pressing the barrel open and inserting a flare *(left)*; close it again. Cock the pistol by pulling the hammer back *(below, left)*; aim it up at a 45° angle, forward of any boat or plane in sight, and pull the trigger *(below, right)*. The parachute-held flare burns for 20 seconds, and on a clear night can be seen for 20 miles. Another type, without parachute, lasts six seconds. Hand-held flares can be seen for only a mile or so.

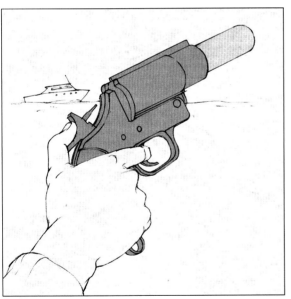

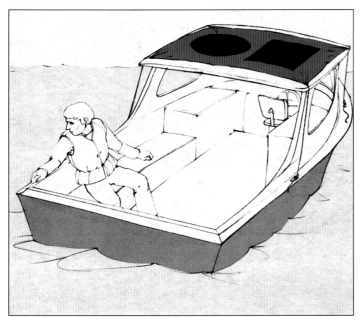

Another effective signal in open water is the international surface-to-air distress flag tied to the cabin roof *(left)*. Developed in Canada, this large panel of fluorescent orange cloth with black ball and square also catches the attention of surface craft if flown from a staff or rigging. Inshore in American waters, sailors still use the traditional distress sign of the U.S. ensign flown upside down.

The simplest visual distress signal, known to both sailors and airmen, is the age-old method of slowly and repeatedly raising and lowering your outstretched arms. To increase the chances of being seen, stand on the highest safe place on your boat and wave pieces of colored cloth or some shiny material such as aluminum foil.

Animal Encounters

55

Animal Encounters

Abandoning Ship

"Rescue may come at any time but not necessarily when you expect it; and even if you give up hope you must never give up trying." Dougal Robertson, author of these words, should know. In June of 1972, two days' sail west of the Galápagos Islands, his schooner, *Lucette*, was unexpectedly hit by a marauding group of killer whales. With three gaping holes in the ship's hull, the boat dipped beneath the waves in less than 60 seconds. Robertson, his wife, three young sons and a 22-year-old passenger faced the Pacific in a life raft and dinghy with only a few simple tools that they had managed to salvage and food and water for only 10 days. They stayed alive for 38 days by a rare blend of grit, ingenuity, and particularly fine seamanship on the part of the skipper.

Rowing back to the Galápagos was impossible because of a strong contrary current. The nearest shipping lanes were 400 miles north, in the area of equatorial calms called the doldrums. Only by reaching this region could the survivors hope to be picked up by a freighter or, failing that, to drift with the current (favorable in those more northerly latitudes) to Central America.

Robertson's primary concern was to keep the two small survival craft upright and moving in the South Pacific swell. As the raft worked in the seaway, a steady internal chafing began to wear holes in the rubber flotation compartments; by the 17th day the raft had sprung so many leaks it had to be abandoned, and the party continued north with the dinghy alone *(pages 58-59)*.

The Robertsons' saga of survival began after three marauding killer whales inexplicably struck their schooner. The voyagers barely had time to launch both an inflatable rubber raft and a fiberglass dinghy. The dinghy had originally been rigged for sailing, but its mast and sail had gone down with the schooner; it held only two oars and 18 pints of fresh water. Aboard the raft was a paddle and an emergency survival kit containing a few dried provisions, some first-aid supplies, a repair kit, and spare line. Before the schooner sank, the Robertsons were also able to salvage a genoa jib, a bag of Bermuda onions, a sewing kit and a vegetable knife from the galley.

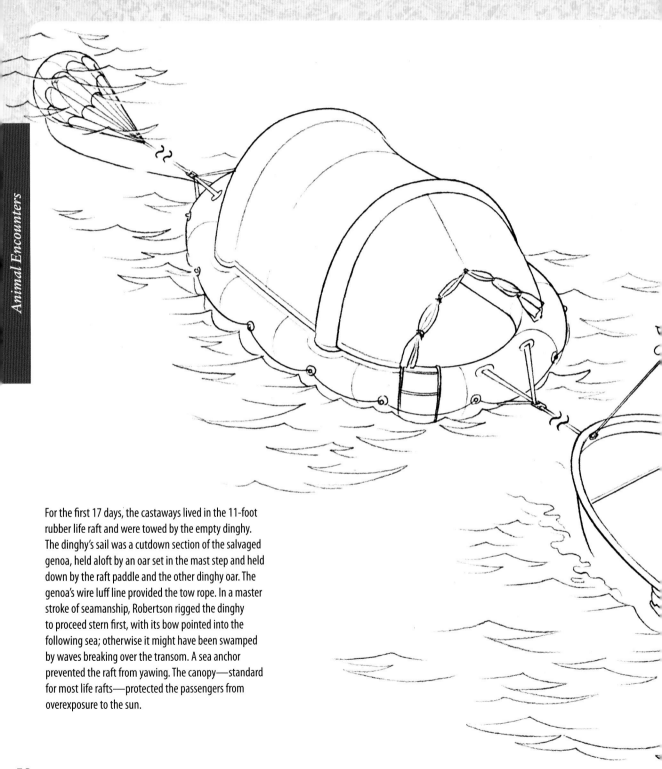

For the first 17 days, the castaways lived in the 11-foot rubber life raft and were towed by the empty dinghy. The dinghy's sail was a cutdown section of the salvaged genoa, held aloft by an oar set in the mast step and held down by the raft paddle and the other dinghy oar. The genoa's wire luff line provided the tow rope. In a master stroke of seamanship, Robertson rigged the dinghy to proceed stern first, with its bow pointed into the following sea; otherwise it might have been swamped by waves breaking over the transom. A sea anchor prevented the raft from yawing. The canopy—standard for most life rafts—protected the passengers from overexposure to the sun.

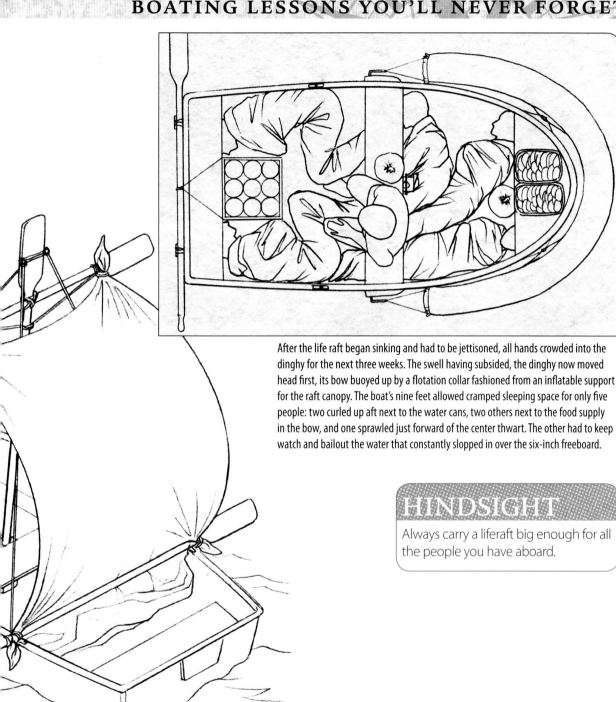

After the life raft began sinking and had to be jettisoned, all hands crowded into the dinghy for the next three weeks. The swell having subsided, the dinghy now moved head first, its bow buoyed up by a flotation collar fashioned from an inflatable support for the raft canopy. The boat's nine feet allowed cramped sleeping space for only five people: two curled up aft next to the water cans, two others next to the food supply in the bow, and one sprawled just forward of the center thwart. The other had to keep watch and bailout the water that constantly slopped in over the six-inch freeboard.

HINDSIGHT

Always carry a liferaft big enough for all the people you have aboard.

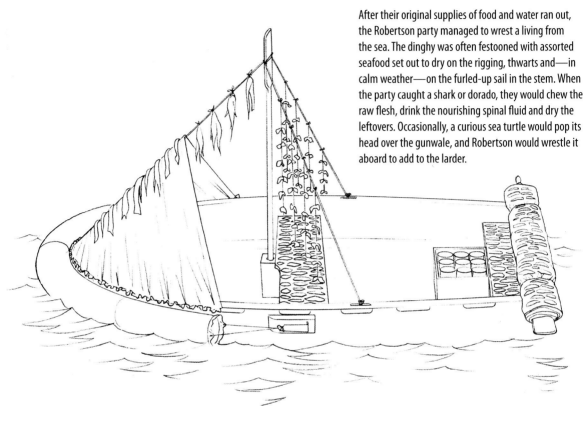

After their original supplies of food and water ran out, the Robertson party managed to wrest a living from the sea. The dinghy was often festooned with assorted seafood set out to dry on the rigging, thwarts and—in calm weather—on the furled-up sail in the stem. When the party caught a shark or dorado, they would chew the raw flesh, drink the nourishing spinal fluid and dry the leftovers. Occasionally, a curious sea turtle would pop its head over the gunwale, and Robertson would wrestle it aboard to add to the larder.

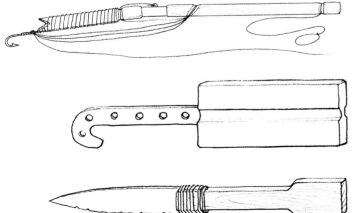

To harvest the seagoing wildlife that accompanied them, the Robertsons improvised a tool kit consisting of an ingeniously rigged gaff for catching fish *(top)*, a hook-nosed knife *(center)* from the raft repair kit and the fragment of a stainless-steel galley knife *(bottom)*, shown with the handle fitted on after the original blade had snapped in two. The gaff, bearing a fishhook at its business end, was spliced together from the handle of a raft paddle and a wooden extension cut from a dinghy thwart. The wire leader for the fishhook was then seized to the wooden extension—leaving the hook itself free to swivel independently and absorb some of the shock when a fish was struck.

38th Day: Rescue

17th Day: Raft Abandoned

7th Day: Ship Sighted

Galápagos Islands

June 15, 1972: *Lucette Sinks*

Pacific Ocean

The route to rescue began with Lucette's sinking 200 miles west of the Galápagos and proceeded first north and then east for 1,000 miles, assisted by the trade winds, the Humboldt Current and crosscurrents in the doldrums. Since he had no chart or compass, Robertson relied on the sun and stars to find direction, and on current speed and wind strength to determine boat speed. He noted each day's estimated position on a scrap of paper, along with major events: a heartbreaking moment on the seventh day when the castaways sighted a freighter steaming past; the sinking of the raft on the 17th day; and finally the rescue by the Japanese fishing boat Toka Maru II.

Refuge on a Raft

For any boat that occasionally ventures offshore from coastal waters or on the Great Lakes, where getting lost can mean days on open water, a heavy-duty life raft like that shown here can be vital to survival. Most cruising boats also carry or tow a conventional dinghy. But dinghies are not designed to carry people for any length of time, and tend to capsize easily. A well-designed raft, however, can last for months in mid-ocean.

A typical life raft is made of a heavy rubberized fabric in a bright, attention-getting color, and includes a permanently attached canopy to protect the crew from the elements. A CO_2 cartridge can inflate the raft in 20-40 seconds.

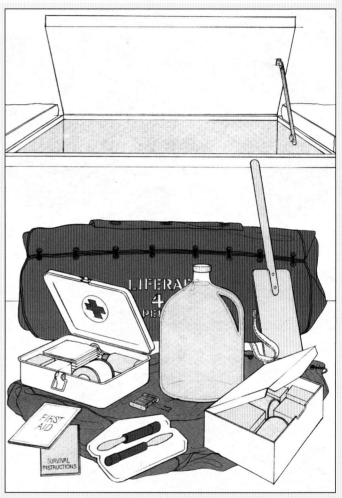

Arranged around a packed raft shown outside its seat locker are items for long-term survival—food (in the box above), water, a fishing kit, an extra paddle, a first-aid kit and book, and flares *(center, bottom)*. Such equipment should be kept in a duffel bag and stowed with the raft. A crew abandoning ship should have a well-rehearsed plan for loading the raft with as much other gear as possible: flashlights, a Very pistol, a radio beacon, navigational equipment, as much extra food and water as can be stowed, blankets, and a change of clothing. Plastic bags for keeping equipment dry are also a good idea, as is reading matter; long hours at sea can be boring as well as frightening.

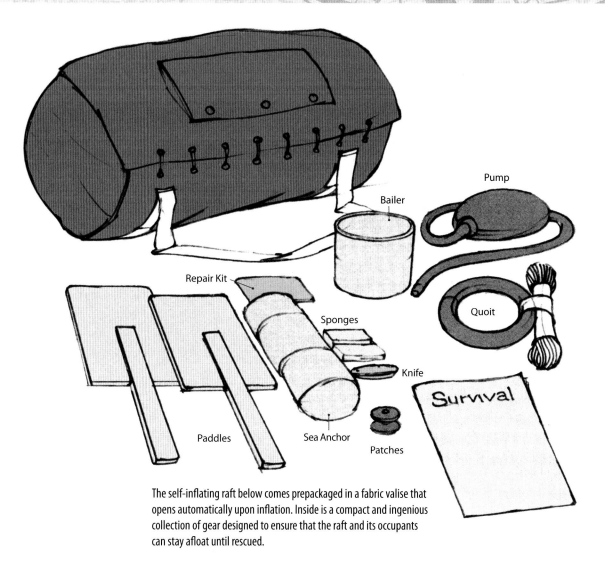

Pump

Bailer

Repair Kit

Sponges

Quoit

Knife

Paddles

Sea Anchor

Patches

Survival

The self-inflating raft below comes prepackaged in a fabric valise that opens automatically upon inflation. Inside is a compact and ingenious collection of gear designed to ensure that the raft and its occupants can stay afloat until rescued.

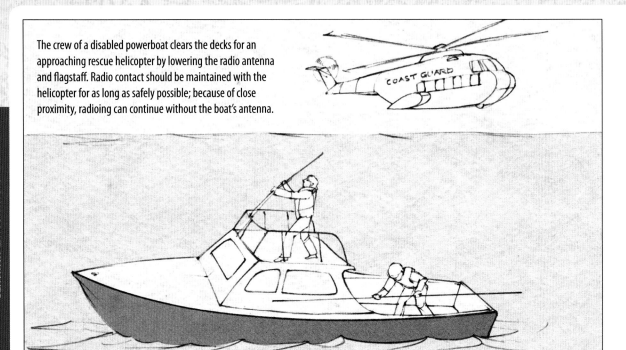

The crew of a disabled powerboat clears the decks for an approaching rescue helicopter by lowering the radio antenna and flagstaff. Radio contact should be maintained with the helicopter for as long as safely possible; because of close proximity, radioing can continue without the boat's antenna.

Rescue by Air

When a disabled boat begins to founder, the skipper faces the grim necessity of leaving it. Long before this point, he should have called or signaled for help *(pages 50–55)*, and if his boat is radio equipped, he should have described any crew injuries. The Coast Guard and other rescue agencies still use boats close in, but today most evacuations at sea are made by helicopter. It is easier to pluck people from a vessel's deck than to transfer them from one boat to another.

Skipper and crew should wait aboard the craft as long as possible. People on a sinking boat are safer, more comfortable and easier to locate than people bobbing in the water. On arrival, the helicopter will hover low over the boat, its rotors creating a powerful downdraft. Therefore all rigging and lines must be secured so as not to hamper the rescue. When in position, the helicopter lowers a rescue basket to pick up people, one at a time.

When the metal rescue basket is lowered, crew members should stand clear until it touches the deck. These baskets carry a heavy charge of static electricity built up by air friction against the whirring rotors, and only after the basket has reached the deck and released its charge is it safe to handle.

HINDSIGHT

Stay on a sinking boat until you have no choice as it is much easier to find someone on a boat than in the water.

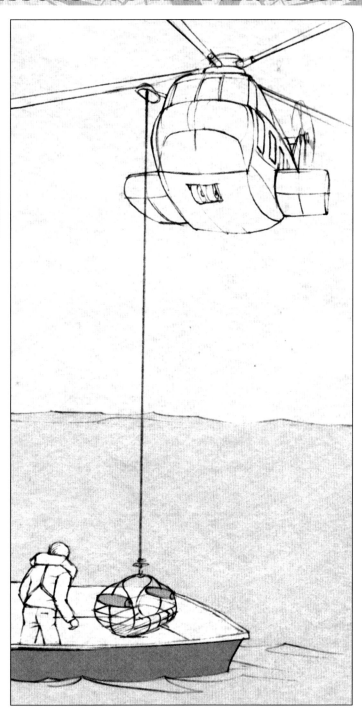

Animal Encounters

Animal Encounters

If kept from working close overhead by the mast of a sailboat, the helicopter drops a trail line weighted with a sandbag. While one crewman grabs the line, the other holds the boom clear. The helicopter then maneuvers to one side and lowers the rescue basket, which is hauled in with the trail line.

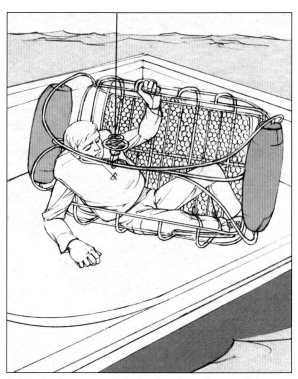

An injured sailor eases into the basket after tilting it for access. If the rescue basket is needed on another part of the boat, it can be unfastened; but the boat's crew should hold the loose line or let it dangle. The line must never be secured to the boat, lest the connection restrict the helicopter.

An overboard sailor swims to the rescue basket, which is held up by flotation devices. The sailor must enter quickly, since the rotors' wind whips up waves that can impede him. Because the basket is mostly submerged, the sailor can arrange himself inside while floating, before being lifted up.

Snug inside the rescue basket, the man being evacuated gives the thumbs-up signal, the sign that he is ready to be raised to the helicopter. He must be sure he is entirely inside the device before giving the signal or he risks falling out of the basket as it is drawn from the water. Once in the helicopter, the survivor should remain in the basket until instructed to leave—hatch doors may have to be closed before he can safely emerge.

CHAPTER 3:

Avoiding the Rocks

The nautical chart is an essential tool for any boatman, whether he is setting off for new waters or cruising along a familiar coastline whose piloting pitfalls may be too numerous to keep in mind. With a chart, no helmsman need ever encounter the unexpected. By using the chart and referring to its numbers and symbols, they would know as they neared land that water depth here decreases from an average of 11 fathoms to two or less, and that the bottom near shore is alternately covered with rocks and anchor-snagging kelp. To orient themselves as they steered toward a desired anchorage, they could establish their position by taking compass bearings. In short, the chart could tell these seamen where they were, where to sail, and where not to sail.

Such vital information is available through charts meticulously prepared by government agencies for all boating areas in the United States. Hundreds of new, or revised, charts are published each year, and well over a million are sold annually to recreational boatmen or accessed for free at www.nauticalcharts. noaa.gov. But even though a chart may be absolutely accurate at the time that it is published and sold, the sea bottom and shorelines are constantly changing—through wave action, wrecks, and the sweep of tidal currents. A boatman should always keep his navigation nook stocked with the most recent charts; thus he avoids such dangers as ramming the hulk of an oil tanker recently sunk or running aground in a channel that shoaled in after his obsolete chart was updated.

However, since the waters move more quickly than government cartographers, the boatman should also consult a weekly government publication called *Notice to Mariners*, which announces recent discoveries affecting navigational safety and can be used to supplement and correct chart information between publications. Two other vital publications for chart users are the Coast Pilot, which gives detailed sailing directions for various areas, and a pamphlet called, curiously enough, *Chart No. 1*, which catalogues every chart symbol used by United States mariners.

Foggy shoals like the one here are particularly hazardous to unprepared boaters.

Lost at Sea

On a summer day not long ago, a man surprised his family by arriving home towing behind his car a beautiful little 15-foot outboard motorboat. The next weekend he and his wife and their two children drove to the coast. In high spirits they launched their new craft into the calm waters of a secluded cove.

A gentle breeze was blowing off the land, and by the time they were a mile or so out into the bay, the sea had risen to a lively ripple—nothing to alarm a sailor, but unsettling to these novices. They turned back, into the wind and sea, whereupon the boat began to rock disconcertingly, while a splash or two of water came aboard. Suddenly the engine stalled, and within minutes what had begun as a carefree outing became a matter of survival.

The whole family was soon so seasick that no one in the boat could try to restart the engine. They had no oars, no sail, and no idea of how to jury-rig a facsimile of either one from the gear they had aboard. At sundown the air turned cold; they had not even brought any warm clothing. Furthermore, they had nothing with which to signal for help, and they had told no one ashore that they were putting out from that lonely beach.

Twelve hours later they were picked up by a passing ship, seven or eight miles out in the ocean, cold, wet, miserable—and far wiser about the moods of the sea. In a frightening but fortunately nonfatal experience, they had learned the primary rule that pleasure, even survival, on the water depends on a combination of knowledge, preparedness, vigilance and coolheadedness. These qualities, honed to a fine edge by constant practice, define the art of seamanship. By exercising any one of them, the family could have had a pleasant spin. Without them they were—almost literally—lost.

BOATING LESSONS YOU'LL NEVER FORGET

The waters of a rising tide foam around the pilings of a causeway spanning a narrow New Jersey canal— evidence of a racing tidal current that would be impossible for a slow-moving boat to make any way against. In fact, a small boat could easily be pinned to the pilings by such a strong current—and possibly even be capsized.

HINDSIGHT

Be sure to dress for changes in weather.

A whirlpool, one of the most frightening of oceanic disturbances, occurs where powerful tidal currents move rapidly over an uneven bottom or through a narrow passage. A small boat could be spun about, and possibly even capsized, by this one—which measures at least six feet across its ominous vortex—off the Brittany coast in the Gulf of Saint-Malo.

These powerful waves, surging up an otherwise calm stretch of England's Severn River, are in the van of a tidal bore. This unusual current phenomenon results when an exceptionally high tide builds up against—and then sweeps over—a sand bar or other obstruction at the mouth of the river. Bores occur in a number of tidal rivers, and can reach heights of 30 feet. In 325 B.C., a bore on the Indus River scattered Alexander the Great's ships and panicked his seamen.

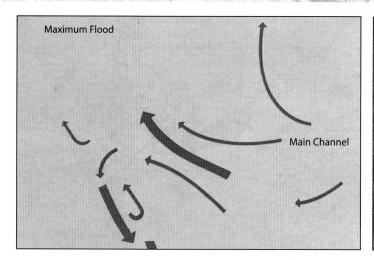

Maximum Flood

Main Channel

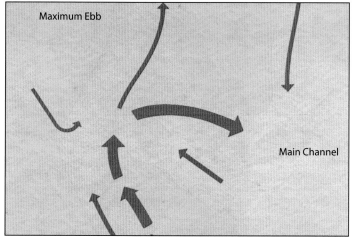

Maximum Ebb

Main Channel

Avoiding the Rocks

The complex behavior of tidal currents is illustrated above in two simplified charts of a part of Puget Sound, Washington. One shows currents during the peak flow of flood tide; the other shows ebb tide currents some six hours later. The current's direction, or set, is affected by landforms; countercurrents and eddies tend to occur where the waters wash around a point or island. The speed, or drift, of the current is often strongest *(heavy arrows)* in narrow passages and is weaker *(light arrows)* in open areas.

Two views of a buoy anchored in a coastal inlet give graphic proof of a current change. In the top picture, the flooding current sweeps the buoy in its own direction, leaning it over and causing a swirl downcurrent. Four hours later the same buoy is tilted the other way by the ebbing current as it flows seaward.

73

A perfectly defined sequence of waves, generated by winds far out at sea, rolls in toward shore. Usually, local winds, crosscurrents and other wave trains cause patterns to be more erratic than this one.

The most varied—and potentially hazardous—of the sea's motions are its waves. Though often they do no more than pucker the water in harmless ripples, they can build up into towering, destructive crests. In 1966 during a North Atlantic gale, one giant wave smashed into the Italian liner *Michelangelo*, shattering windows 81 feet above the waterline.

Most waves, big or small, are generated by the wind, which presses on the water's surface, causing it to undulate. These undulations march along in a regular pattern of ridges called a wave train *(diagram, opposite)*, which may travel hundreds of miles across the open sea. Usually the wave train meets other waves moving in other directions, so most seas become hodgepodges of various wave sequences. Nevertheless, all waves behave according to basic physical laws, and exhibit the family characteristics shown below.

If a wave is high enough, for example, strong winds will force the top of its crest to curl over and break. At sea under stormy conditions, the tops may break when wave heights reach anywhere from 15 to 25 feet. In addition, the entire wave will break whenever its height becomes too great in proportion to its length, which usually occurs when swells approach shore. In shallow water, waves drag along the bottom, so that they slow up and jam together. With the distances between the crests thus shortened, the waves tumble over and collapse—fair warning to the boatman to stay clear.

A stylized profile of a wave train illustrates the basic characteristics of all waves. Wave length is measured from the top of one crest to the top of the next; wave height is the distance from the bottom of a trough to the top of an adjacent crest. The ratio of length to height varies enormously depending on the strength of the wind and how long it has been blowing. Also the depth of the water is a factor in wave behavior: when depth is less than half the distance between crests, the waves become slower and steeper.

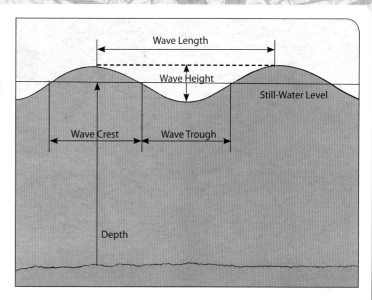

Wave Length

Wave Height

Still-Water Level

Wave Crest   Wave Trough

Depth

Avoiding the Rocks

A wave breaking across an inlet presents a serious hazard to boatmen. Wind-driven swells roll in from the sea, begin to crest as they reach the shallow water near the inlet's mouth, and break as they move through the narrow space inside the jetty in the background. Unless a skipper is skilled at maneuvering through cresting seas, he should anchor outside the inlet until conditions moderate.

Confused, uncomfortable wave conditions like those above occur when the tidal current and wind direction clash. Here the tide is flooding into a bay while the wind is blowing offshore. The resulting chop looks a bit like waves caused by shallows, and might well dismay a boatman coming upon them suddenly; but though they may bounce a boat around, these waves are not dangerous.

Curls of surf breaking across an isolated patch of water are a sure sign of a sand bar or other shoal close to the surface. Even small waves will break when the water becomes shallow enough so that the lower part of the wave train drags along the bottom, causing the crests to rise up, roll over, and collapse.

Mountainous waves like those above form when a strong, steady wind blows for days on end from a constant direction over a wide fetch of ocean. A 45-knot gale, for example, could build up waves 30 feet high. Such mid-ocean giants, however, present less danger to a seaman than do breaking combers such as those above, cresting over a coral reef in the Cocos Islands south of Sumatra in the Indian Ocean.

A Revealing Perspective

A chart gives a sea-level mariner a revealing overhead perspective of the nautical landscape along a given stretch of navigable water. The dominant element tends to be the coastline of any land mass in the area. These coastlines, along with features such as reefs, are rendered with painstaking accuracy, as can be seen by comparing the chart opposite with the photograph of the same region at right.

The photograph depicts parts of two small islands in the Virgin group, a popular cruising ground for Caribbean boatmen. The chart reproduces their coastlines, detailing each bend, point and notch of the islands' coves and promontories. Offshore, the chart portrays rock formations, the surrounding shallows and navigable deep water, with a record of water depths in feet at significant points.

The chart maker's art, interpreting waterway characteristics by means of overhead perspective, also conveys a wealth of other detailed information (shown on the following pages) on shorelines and sea bottom—information that a helmsman must have to navigate safely.

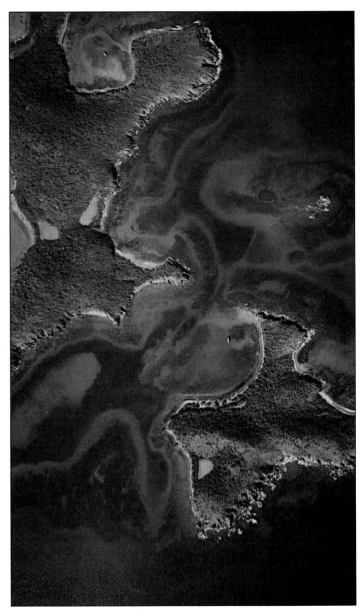

The aerial photograph above, taken at 6,000 feet, was used by cartographers to chart a section of Great and Little St. James, Virgin Islands. Ragged lines of cliffs, defined by breakers, alternate with smooth beaches along the coastlines. A profusion of rocks, particularly off the southern shore of the smaller island, poses navigational hazards. The two white specks in the coves at the top and center of the picture are anchored boats.

This chart of Great and Little St. James islands duplicates all of the coastal characteristics depicted in the aerial photograph opposite, and includes water depths for the entire area. Hatch marks along the shore indicate bluffs, and the chart points out small but dangerous rocks only a few yards from the beach. Wherever possible—as with Welk Rocks to the east of the islands—the cartographers have even drawn the true shapes of the rocks, though they are 25 yards or less in length.

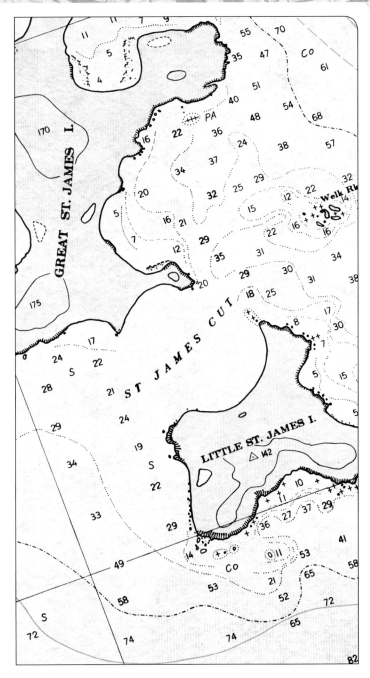

Avoiding the Rocks

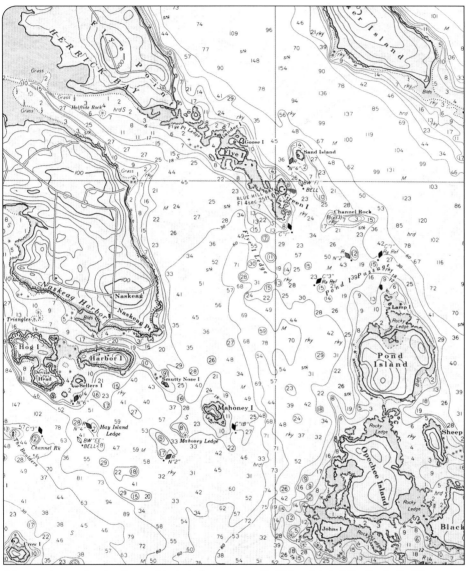

Colors, numbers, and contour lines on this chart of a tricky sailing area off the coast of Maine provide an instant key to water depth. All water less than 18 feet deep at low tide is shown here in blue, depths from 18 to 30 feet in lighter blue, and depths over 30 feet in white. Within the tinted areas, contour lines at prescribed intervals help define the depth differences. Each contour line is labeled in italics to show its depth, as can be seen by 12-, 18-, 30- and 60-foot notations on the contour lines just north of Pond Island. Frequent soundings, noted here in feet, give depth readings at mean low water.

The Underwater Terrain

The most vital service a chart performs is to describe the territory beneath the skipper's hull. Using a combination of numbers, color codes, underwater contour lines and a system of abbreviations and symbols, the chart tells a pilot all he needs to know about an area's undersea topography, including where he can safely venture and the sections he should avoid.

Most of the numbers on the chart represent measurements of the water's depth at mean low tide, taken at the spot by a hydrographic vessel. These soundings maybe either in feet or in fathoms (a fathom equals six feet); the chart's legend will indicate which unit is used. Contour lines, which connect points of roughly equal depth, profile the bottom's shape; the lines are either numbered *(chart, opposite)* or coded *(chart, right)* according to depth. Color shadings also indicate depth, with the shallowest areas in the darkest tint. Rocks and reefs, and various other characteristics of the bottom, are marked by either standardized symbols or abbreviations, as described at right.

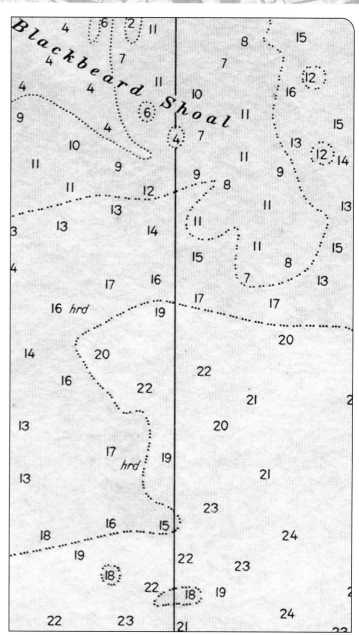

On some charts, as in this excerpt showing Blackbeard Shoal off the Georgia coast, the depth of each contour line is indicated by a system of dots. And even though the individual soundings are in feet, the dots refer to fathoms. Thus lines of single dots enclose areas of one fathom *(six feet)* or less, while lines of double and triple dots indicate depths of two and three fathoms respectively.

Avoiding the Rocks

81

Wrecks, Rocks, Reefs

Cartographers choose from a selection of stylized notations, like the ones shown below, to indicate underwater hazards. A sunken wreck, for example, may be shown either by a symbol or by an abbreviation plus a number that gives the wreck's depth. A dotted line around any symbol calls special attention to its hazardous nature. Since slightly different symbols often indicate the same hazard , the boatman should consult the complete list in the pamphlet entitled *Chart No. 1*, published by the National Ocean Survey and available at both the NOS distribution office and most marine-supply outlets.

Sunken wrecks (abbreviation: Wk); a number indicates precise depth in feet at mean low water.

A partly submerged wreck, showing part of its superstructure or hull at mean low water.

Sunken rocks (abbreviation: Rk); a number indicates the precise depth at mean low water.

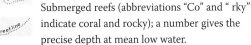

Submerged reefs (abbreviations "Co" and " rky" indicate coral and rocky); a number gives the precise depth at mean low water.

Rocks that are covered at high tide and uncovered at low; height is given in feet above mean low water. Parentheses enclose uncovered height.

Rocks awash at high water.

Rocks awash at low water.

A rock never covered by water, with height above mean high water.

Coral reefs located offshore that are uncovered at mean low water.

An area fouled by wreckage, rocks, or coral.

Bottom Quality

A system of cartographer's abbreviations, used alone or in combination, describes the composition of the bottom, allowing a skipper to pick the best holding ground for his anchor. He should look for hard sand (hrd S), for example, to hold him securely, trying to avoid a rocky (rky) or weed-choked (Wd) bottom that could snag his anchor or allow it to drag.

S	sand	**sft**	soft
M	mud	**hrd**	hard
G	gravel	**stk**	sticky
Sh	shells	**rky**	rocky
Wd	seaweed	**gy**	gray
Grs	grass	**br**	brown

Clear Warnings of Shoal Waters

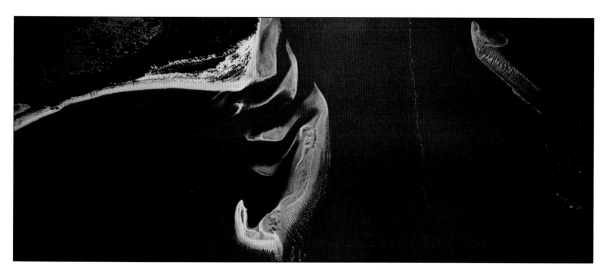

At the inlet to St. Catherines Sound, Georgia, shifting sand bars—which are seen in this aerial photograph as pale slashes—flank the channel and create a constant threat to navigation. But the color codes and symbols on the chart below (marked off with a blue rectangle corresponding to the area covered in the photo) give pilots clear warning of the hazards. The sand bars show up as green areas enclosed by dotted lines, indicating they are uncovered at low tide. Breakers are labeled; hard bottom is indicated by the abbreviation "hrd." "Middle Ground" is the name of a shoal just inside the inlet.

Avoiding the Rocks

The Look of the Coast

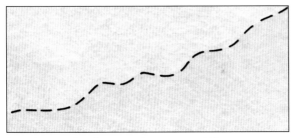

Approximate outline of unsurveyed coast at mean high water.

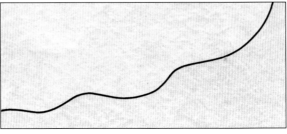

Exact outline of a surveyed coast at mean high water.

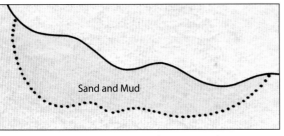

Sand and mud flats, adjacent to a coast, that are exposed at mean low water.

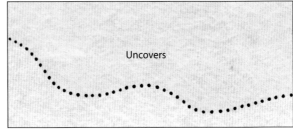

Any area, adjacent to the coast or detached from it, that uncovers at mean low water.

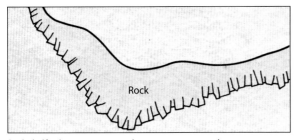

Rock shelf, adjacent to a coast, that uncovers at mean low water.

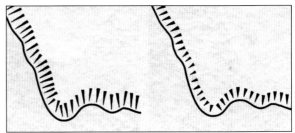

Coastal cliffs; the longer hatch marks at left signify higher elevation.

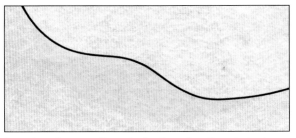

Approximate low-water line, as in situations where the water level varies from tide to tide.

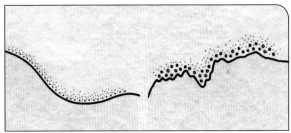

Coastal lowlands; sandy at left, rocky at right.

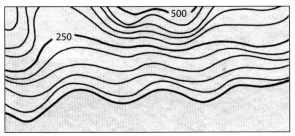

High coastal hills; contour lines indicate elevations.

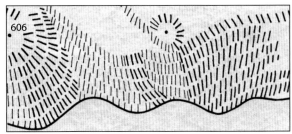

Steeply inclined coastline; hatch marks are drawn in the direction of the slopes.

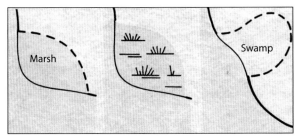

Marsh or swamp; either labeled as such or indicated by a symbol (middle).

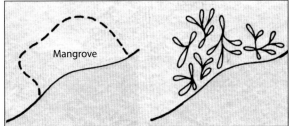

Mangrove area; either labeled or indicated by a symbol.

Symbols for Landmarks

Besides a knowledge of the underwater terrain, the mariner needs a clear representation of the coastal landscape; the chart provides it. Coastlines are depicted at both high tide and low, inland topography is defined, and any landmark that might help a navigator fix his position is noted and labeled.

Some of the drafting techniques used to portray the shape and character of coastal areas are shown at right. Contour lines or hatch marks designate slopes and cliffs.

Dots or speckles along the shoreline indicate a sandy or boulder-strewn beach. And green tints denote areas that are uncovered when the tide goes out.

A variety of dots, circles, and other symbols *(pages 84-85)* give the locations of prominent landmarks. And on some charts—most notably those for foreign waters—churches, temples and mosques merit their own symbols. Samples are shown on page 87, along with stylized drawings of the buildings themselves.

A Key to Prominent Checkpoints

To pinpoint the location of high, man-made landmarks such as water towers, smokestacks, flagpoles and radio beacons, cartographers use the standard symbol of a dot surrounded by a circle. A notation next to the symbol defines the landmark's precise nature—whether, for example, it is a large domed roof or small cupola—as explained in the table of selected landmarks below. If the dot is omitted, the notation will be given in lower-case type—indicating that the landmark's position is approximate.

⊙ **CHY**	The chimney of a building; the building is not charted, because the more visible chimney gives a navigator a better bearing.	⊙ **GAB**	A prominent gable on the roof of a building, providing a more precise bearing than would the building as a whole.	⊙ **TR**	A tower that is part of a larger building.
⊙ **STACK**	A tall industrial smokestack.	⊙ **FP**	A free-standing flagpole.	⊙ **R TR**	A radio tower—either a tall pole or a tall scaffolded structure for elevating radio antennas.
⊙ **S'PIPE**	A standpipe or a tall cylindrical structure, such as a water tower, whose height is greater than its diameter.	⊙ **FS**	A flagstaff attached to a building.	⊙ **R MAST**	A radio mast—a relatively short pole or scaffolded structure for elevating radio antennas.
⊙ **TANK**	A water tank that is elevated above the ground by means of a tall skeletal framework.	⊙ **DOME**	The dome of a building. If the building is well known, its name may appear in parentheses; e.g., DOME (STATE HOUSE).	⊙ **LORAN TR**	A loran tower—a tall, slender structure, braced with guy wires, for elevating loran antennas.
⊙ **MON**	A monument, such as an obelisk or statue.	⊙ **CUP**	A cupola—a small dome-shaped turret atop a building.	⊙ **TELEM ANT**	The large dish-shaped antenna—known as a telemetry antenna—of a missile tracking station.

Structures Drawn to Scale

For low-lying structures such as piers, ramps, and bridges—and also for buildings and towns—cartographers have developed shorthand representations such as the ones shown here. Thus, various rectangular or triangular shapes may indicate streets with houses along them; old military forts are shown by an outline of their ramparts. Such symbols are drawn to scale, and depict the landmarks as viewed from overhead. Like all landmark symbols used on nautical charts, these are listed in *Chart No. 1*.

Ecumenical Signposts

Spires make handy landmarks. On United States charts, they are shown merely by a circle. But for foreign waters, chart makers distinguish between religions with the special symbols at left below (the drawings at right are supplied here for convenient identification).

⊙ Spire	Spire	
†	Christian church	
⊠	Temple	
⊠	Pagoda	
Λ	Mosque	
	Minaret	

A grid of streets representing a city or town.

A dam. The tooth-edged line represents the dam structure; the lines below, the runoff.

A water-front ramp; broken lines indicate the portion submerged at mean low tide.

Groups of adjoining buildings; large rectangles are usually shaded, small ones blank.

A military fort.

A pair of jetties; broken lines mark the extent of their under water foundations.

Individual buildings. Larger symbols are shaded, small ones filled in or left blank.

Short parallel docks projecting out into the water from a curved bulkhead.

A long single pier projecting into the water.

A bascule drawbridge, whose sections swing up like the gates at a railroad crossing.

A swinging drawbridge. The center section turns upon a central pier.

Avoiding the Rocks

A Mariner's Match-up

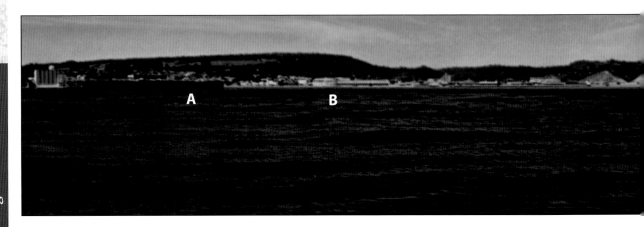

Matching chart symbols to landmarks, a boatman traveling past Santa Cruz Harbor in Monterey Bay, California, can find his position by identifying prominent man-made features on shore. The large letters on the photograph above identify: (A) an 800-yard-long pier, (B) a conspicuous domed structure, (C) a stretch of buildings, and (D) the mouth of a small boat harbor. All four are reproduced (with duplicate letters for easy recognition) on the chart in stylized symbols: a long yellow ramp for the pier, a circle and dot for the dome, a grid for the buildings, and two broken lines for the harbor channel.

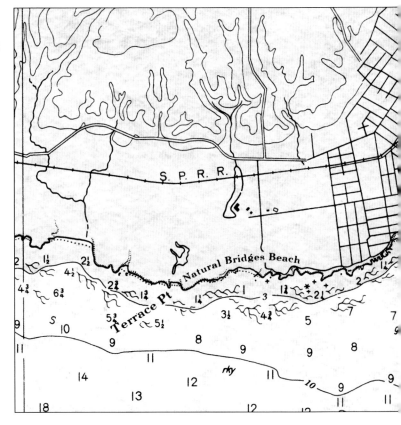

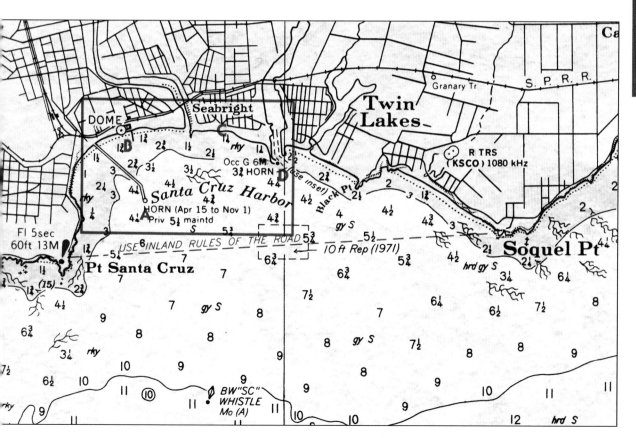

The Rules of The Road

In days not long past, a mariner could roam for weeks on end, rarely sighting another craft, free to think of nothing but water, wind, and the surging power of his vessel. Now all too often that exhilarating sense of freedom is blotted out by the looming presence of another boat, perhaps one as formidable as the giant tanker bearing down on the runabout at right. With the enormous increase in both pleasure craft and commercial vessels—some 900,000 new boats are launched each year in American waters—the boatman today must be as alert to traffic as is any shore-bound motorist. In fact, chugging across such heavily traveled waterways as Puget Sound, Lake Mendota, Wisconsin, or Chesapeake Bay has become the nautical equivalent of maneuvering down Hollywood Boulevard on Saturday night. For example, in 1974 two unlighted powerboats, out for a two a.m. ride on a Pennsylvania lake, collided at high speed. The larger boat sank, but its lone operator swam safely ashore; the skipper of the smaller boat was killed on the spot. In Buttermilk Channel, off New York City, an 18-foot powerboat was sliced in two by a towing cable between a tugboat and a barge. Although they were properly lighted, the pilot of the powerboat mistakenly decided that the tug and the barge were not connected. He and his three passengers paid for his mistake with their lives.

Such accidents take more than 1,300 lives and injure nearly 1,500 other victims each year in the United States. The statistics would be infinitely grimmer but for a compendium of laws, commonly called the Rules of the Road, which govern maritime traffic all over the world, and cover almost every conceivable kind of nautical confrontation.

HINDSIGHT
Always give tugboats a wide berth.

Prudently waiving his right of way over the huge vessel approaching on his left, an imperiled powerboat skipper applies the rule of common sense and guns his craft out of danger.

Avoiding the Rocks

Collision Courses: Power

In almost every waterborne confrontation the Rules designate one vessel as having the right of way; this privileged vessel is required to maintain its course and speed (indicated by arrows on these pages). The other boat is known as the burdened vessel—tinted on these pages—and it must get out of the way. Its best course is also indicated by an arrow. The judgment as to which boat is burdened is based on a concept of relative position, sometimes referred to as zones of approach *(below)*.

In addition to taking proper action, powerboats in potential collision situations must signal their intent with blasts of a whistle, horn, or other sound signal. These warning sounds are of three kinds: long, of 8 to 10 seconds' duration, to be used when leaving a dock or going around a bend; prolonged, 4 to 6 seconds, for use in fog; and short, 1 second, used to signify (and acknowledge) intent to turn right (one blast) or left (two blasts), or to go into reverse (three blasts). A series of short blasts warns of danger.

In a potential nose-to-nose collision, each boat is in the other's so-called meeting zone. Therefore both are burdened, and must give way. The Rules state they should turn so as to pass port side to port side, as cars do on the highway. A single, short whistle blast signals this maneuver; giving a similar short blast is the proper response of assent.

Zones of Approach

Rules of the Road divide the water around a boat into zones of approach. If another vessel appears in a boat's meeting zone or in its right-hand crossing rout, the latter must give way.

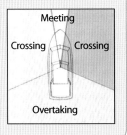

Meeting
Crossing   Crossing
Overtaking

Sometimes in a meeting situation, such as the one at left, when two boats are approaching starboard bow to starboard bow, but far enough apart so there is no danger of collision, they can legally pass each other starboard to starboard. Each acknowledges the situation and intent with two short blasts.

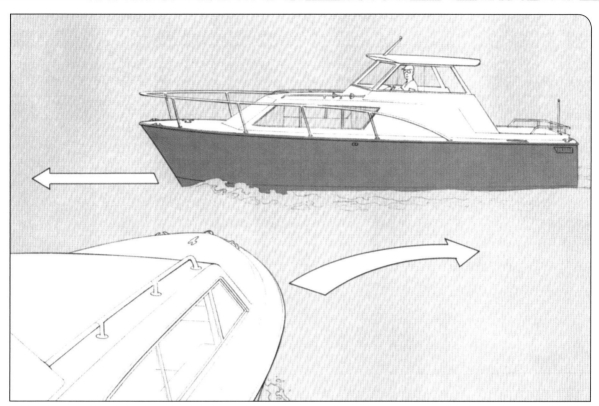

In the crossing situation shown above, the boat in the foreground has the other in its danger zone, i.e., on the right-hand side. No whistle signals are required, but as the burdened vessel, the foreground boat must get out of the way of the other—best done here by turning right. The privileged boat must maintain its course and speed.

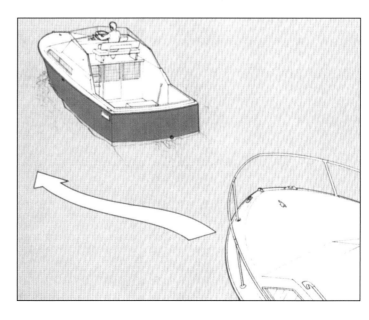

A boat that is overtaking another from behind is always burdened and must stay clear. The usual course is to signal two short whistle blasts, turn left and leave the other boat to starboard. The overtaken boat replies in kind—or if there is danger ahead, warns the other to wait with four short blasts.

Collision Courses: Sail

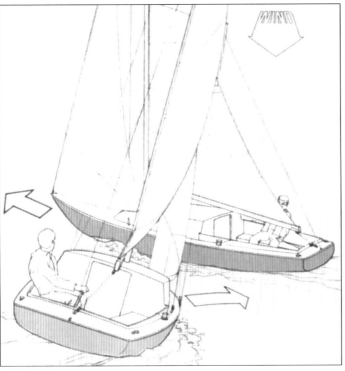

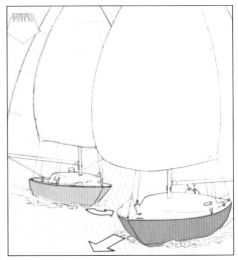

Starboard tack also has right of way when two sailboats running before the wind on opposite tacks are converging on the same point. However, should one boat approach another from behind, as here, it then is overtaking and must keep out of the other's way regardless of which tack it is sailing on.

When two close-hauled sailboats converge, starboard tack always has right of way. The boat on the port tack (i.e., with the wind coming over its port side) must stay clear—by turning to pass astern of the other *(above)*, by tacking onto a new course or by luffing up until the other has passed by.

In normal meeting and crossing situations, sail has right of way over power. Exceptions occur when a sailboat overtakes a powerboat—and therefore must keep clear—and when the sailboat meets certain power vessels that are operating with limited maneuverability. A sailboat under auxiliary power also loses its privilege over powerboats even if the sailboat's canvas is hoisted.

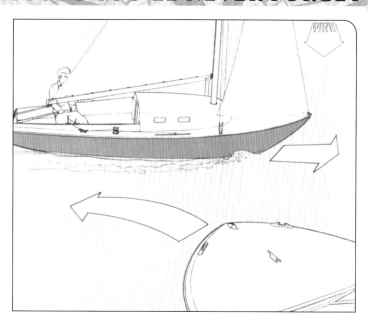

When two boats are sailing along side by side on the same tack, the boat to leeward—the one farthest from the source of the wind—has the right of way. The boat on the windward side must avoid bearing down on the other, even if that means luffing up or coming about to the other tack to keep clear.

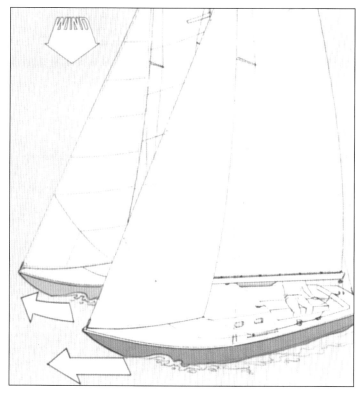

On inland waters an exception to starboard tack right of way occurs when the boat sailing before the wind on the starboard tack meets one close-hauled: the craft running free must give way even if the other is on port tack. This rule is a relic of the days of square riggers, which were hard to maneuver upwind.

An International Variant

Under International Rules a sailboat on the starboard tack has the right of way even when it is running free and encounters a boat close-hauled on the port tack. This overall privilege to the starboard-tack boat (except when it is overtaking) is also accorded to sailboats in competition under the racing rules of the North American Yacht Racing Union.

Intrusions on the Fairway

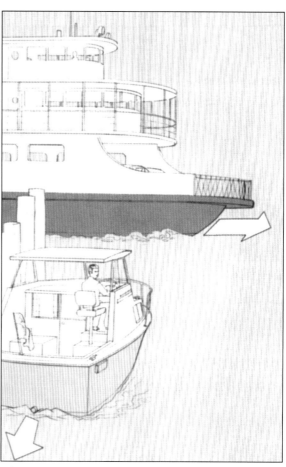

A boat moving in a channel—or fairway—normally has the right of way over all boats leaving a dock or berth. The docked powerboat shown above must give one long whistle blast before backing—and must stop if the boat in the fairway warns of a collision by sounding four or more short blasts.

A ferryboat is the only vessel that enjoys the right of way when docking or moving out into the fairway. Though no formal regulation specifies this privilege, the ferry's inherent need to embark and dock repeatedly and on schedule has resulted in a tacit agreement among seamen to give ferries the right of way.

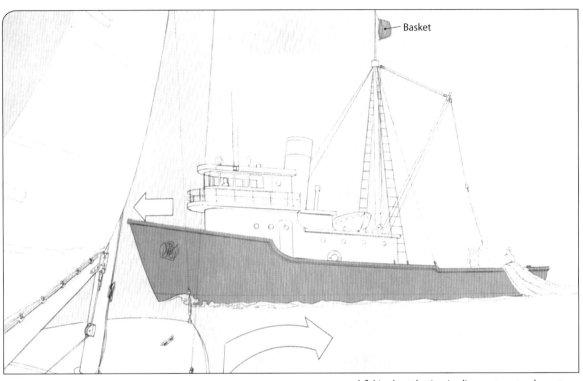

Basket

A fishing boat that is using lines, nets, or trawls must display a so-called day shape *(see above)* in the form of a basket, warning other vessels to keep clear. Under both Inland and International Rules, a sailboat has no right of way over such a fisherman and, as shown here, must turn aside for him. The same rules ban fishing craft from obstructing fairways or channels regularly used by other boats.

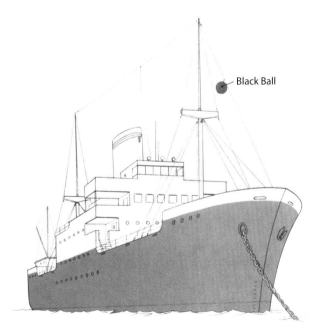

Black Ball

Between sunrise and sunset, Inland Rules require a vessel of over 65 feet anchored in a fairway to hoist into its rigging a black sphere at least two feet in diameter. Called day shapes, the sphere and the basket shown above are among several conformations hoisted in daylight to identify vessels with limited or no maneuverability, and to warn other boats to keep clear of them.

The two powerboats, above, approaching each other at a bend in a river, are following the prescribed procedure of keeping well to the right of midchannel whenever practicable. Upon approaching a bend or curve that obscures visibility, a powerboat must signal with one long blast of its whistle when within half a mile of the bend. Any boat approaching from the other side must answer with a similar blast, confirming its presence. When in sight of each other the two will exchange passing signals.

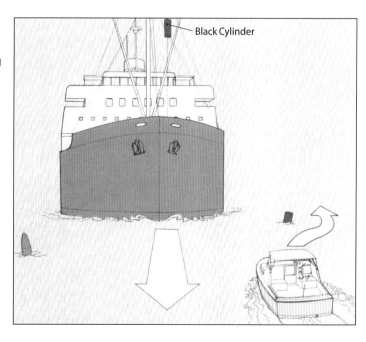

Black Cylinder

The launch in this illustration is turning to the right, out of the channel and out of the way of an approaching freighter. In so doing the boatman is obeying a very sound canon which specifies that a powerboat under 60 feet long may not hamper the passage, in a channel, of a larger, less maneuverable vessel whose draft forces it to stay in the channel. The larger vessel may also display a day shape in the form of a black cylinder as an indication of limited maneuverability.

Avoiding the Rocks

Narrow Passages

Though the perils of the stormy sea are legendary, well over half of the boating accidents in the United States occur on lakes, canals, and nontidal rivers in perfectly clear weather. The reasons for this unhappy situation are two: the enormous number of small pleasure craft that ply such waters and the fact that a sunny day is a beckoning invitation for everybody to set sail at the same time. Thus the crowded inland waterways on a bright morning are potentially more dangerous to a boatman than a night squall at sea, and navigation in narrow channels, where maneuverability is limited, can be a perilous undertaking—as shown in the illustrations on these pages.

To prevent accidents in these heavily trafficked channels, the various Rules of the Road cover almost any situation a navigator is likely to encounter. However, some of the differences among the four sets of Rules can cause accidents if not thoroughly understood. For example, the Western Rivers and Great Lakes Rules give priority to vessels traveling downstream *(right)*. The other two codes make no distinction with regard to current direction. International and Great Lakes Rules demand five or more whistle blasts as a signal for danger, while Inland and Western Rivers Rules specify a minimum of four. Such differences are slight, but in moments of stress can be significant.

Coping with River Currents

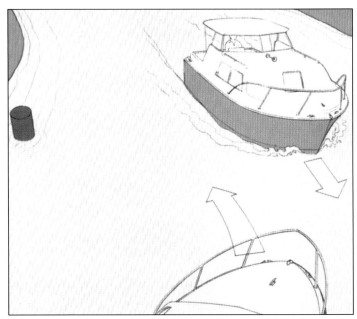

Since Western Rivers Rules favor vessels moving with the current, the cruiser about to cross the starboard bow of the boat moving downstream immediately below must give way—although it would have the right of way in a normal crossing situation.

The best thing a neophyte skipper can do is to memorize those general Rules of the Road that apply to the waters he sails—particularly those having to do with hazardous channel navigation—so that they become second nature. In addition, he will be wise to check the Coast Guard Pilot Rules for any special regulations or guidance; in a constricted channel there is no margin for error.

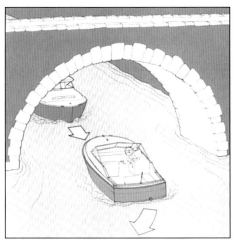

Under Western Rivers Rules, a boat coming downstream toward a bridge has right of way over an ascending boat—even if the latter is already under the bridge. The privileged craft, by sounding the danger signal, can force the other to back clear.

When a fog-bound boat runs aground, International Rules require a special signal: five seconds of rapid bell ringing, preceded and followed by three separate and distinct strokes of the bell at intervals of no more than one minute. Inland Rules make no provision for this situation, but good seamanship dictates the use of this danger signal as a warning to other boats.

A Guide to Fog Signals

Powerboats Underway	Inland: 1 four- to 6-second blast every minute. International: when moving, 1 blast every 2 minutes; when stopped, 2 blasts every 2 minutes. Great Lakes: 3 blasts a minute. Western Rivers: 2 short blasts followed by 1 long a minute.
Sailboats Underway	Inland, International and Great Lakes: starboard tack sounds 1 blast a minute; port tack, 2 a minute; wind abaft the beam, 3 a minute. Western Rivers Rules have no rules for sailboats.
Vessels at Anchor	Inland, International and Western Rivers: rapid ringing of a bell for 5 seconds every minute. International: ships over 350 feet sound a gong and a bell. Great Lakes: a bell every 2 minutes and blasts of 1 short, 2 long, 1 short every 3 minutes.
Towing Vessels	Inland and International: 1 prolonged blast plus 2 short per minute. Great Lakes: a steamer with a raft in tow sounds a whistle per minute. Otherwise the powerboat's underway signal is sounded. Western Rivers: 3 blasts per minute.
Vessels in Tow	Inland: same signal as towing boat. International: if manned, 1 prolonged blast plus 3 short. Great Lakes: 4 bells in groups of 2 every minute. No Western Rivers rule.
Vessels Aground	Inland: no special provision *(see illustration above)*. International: anchor bell with 3 short strokes before and after the signal. Great Lakes: if in a channel, same as anchor signal. Western Rivers Rules: no provision.

Avoiding the Rocks

Fog and Distress Signals

As the charts on these pages indicate, the four major sets of Rules of the Road do not, surprisingly, agree on very many details of their required fog and distress signals. However they are unanimous on a few basic principles. For example, all state that fog signals should be sounded in "fog, mist, falling snow, or heavy rainstorms," and all caution boats in fog to proceed at "moderate" speed, which maritime courts have ruled can mean no forward motion whatsoever in very thick conditions. As an extra caution, International Rules stipulate that these procedures be followed even if a vessel has radar. Under Inland Rules, fog signals are given whenever visibility is reduced to one mile.

Although no Rules so state, a prudent seaman will sound fog signals before entering a fogbank, to alert any nearby vessels that might already be fogbound.

Fog signals are more than simple noises indicating a vessel's presence. When understood they provide other vital information, such as the size and limitation of maneuverability of a boat. They can even help to indicate a boat's specific activity, like which tack a sailboat is on.

In order to make proper fog or distress signals, powerboats must carry a whistle or, in Inland Waters, a siren. Sailboats must have a foghorn and both types of vessels are required to carry an efficient bell. Larger ships—over 350 feet long—must also have a gong or another instrument that is not easily confused with a bell, to alternate with the bell and warn other boats that a big ship is anchored.

Upside Down—and Out

One of the best-known visual distress signals in American waters is an inverted U.S. ensign. However, this signal is not recognized by the Rules, since other maritime nations have flags which appear the same whether right side up or upside down. The Coast Guard recommends arm-waving or other International signals—which are as visible and often quicker than capsizing the ensign.

BOATING LESSONS YOU'LL NEVER FORGET

The devices shown above are commonly used to signal distress. They are a ship's horn, a hand gun *(often called a Very pistol)* which fires brilliant flares into the air, and a hand-held smoke flare. These and other distress signals, recognized under the four Rules of the Road are listed below. But whether authorized or not, a good distress signal is any one that brings help.

How to Call for Help

Signals	Inland Rules	Great Lakes Rules	Western Rivers Rules	International Rules
A continuous sounding with any fog-signaling apparatus	day night	day night	day night	anytime
A gun or other explosive signal fired at intervals of about a minute	day night	day night	day night	anytime
Controlled flames on the vessel (as from a flare, burning tar barrel, etc.)	night	night	night	anytime
A signal consisting of a square flag having above or below it a ball or anything resembling a ball		day	day	anytime
A man standing in a conspicuous position, slowly and repeatedly raising and lowering his outstretched arms	day	day	day	anytime
Rockets or cartridges whose projectiles are red stars fired one at a time at short intervals		night	day night	anytime
The "N" and "C" flags of the International Code hoisted high in a ship's rigging			day	anytime
SOS: signal by radiotelegraphy or other signaling method consisting of the group ... — — — ... in Morse Code				anytime
A radiotelephone signal consisting of the spoken word "Mayday"				anytime
A rocket parachute flare or a hand flare showing a red light				anytime
A smoke signal giving off a volume of orange-colored smoke				anytime

Lights on Inland Waters

The navigation lights of vessels at night convey an astonishing amount of information, and it is vital that the boatman master the meanings of these signals—known also as running lights. The proliferation of pleasure craft and the attendant increased danger of collision make clear nighttime communication essential for survival.

The Rules of the Road carefully spell out the characteristics of each light: its position on the vessel, the required range of visibility, its color and the arc through which it must be visible *(opposite)*. Every sail or power craft is required to carry some combination of these lights that will identify it according to size and type. Some of the commonest regulations of the Inland Rules are shown on this page; the international versions are on page 106.

The vessels in the drawings display only those lights that would be visible to a boatman observing the vessel from the viewpoint shown. In actual situations, the light patterns change as the vessel moves. By learning to read these patterns, a seaman knows in an instant on the darkest night which way a vessel is heading, how big it is and what it is doing. Most important, he knows immediately who has the right of way.

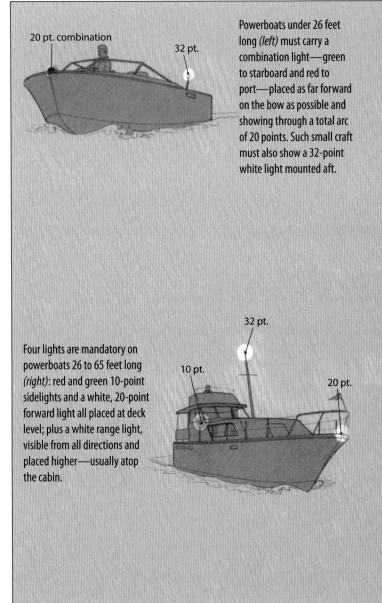

20 pt. combination

32 pt.

Powerboats under 26 feet long *(left)* must carry a combination light—green to starboard and red to port—placed as far forward on the bow as possible and showing through a total arc of 20 points. Such small craft must also show a 32-point white light mounted aft.

32 pt.

10 pt.

20 pt.

Four lights are mandatory on powerboats 26 to 65 feet long *(right)*: red and green 10-point sidelights and a white, 20-point forward light all placed at deck level; plus a white range light, visible from all directions and placed higher—usually atop the cabin.

Avoiding the Rocks

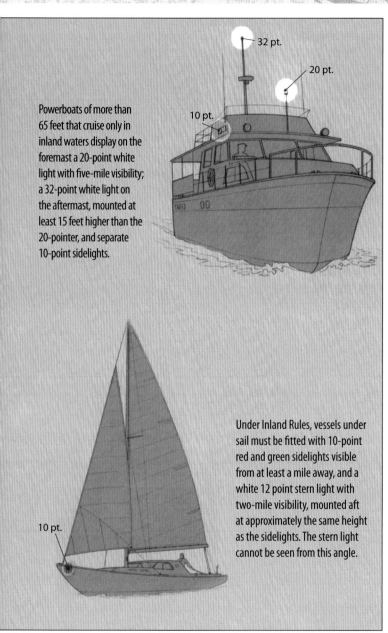

Powerboats of more than 65 feet that cruise only in inland waters display on the foremast a 20-point white light with five-mile visibility; a 32-point white light on the aftermast, mounted at least 15 feet higher than the 20-pointer, and separate 10-point sidelights.

Under Inland Rules, vessels under sail must be fitted with 10-point red and green sidelights visible from at least a mile away, and a white 12 point stern light with two-mile visibility, mounted aft at approximately the same height as the sidelights. The stern light cannot be seen from this angle.

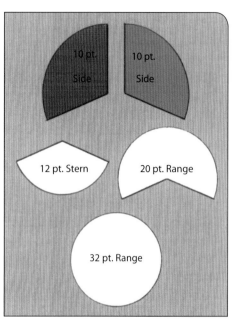

Each navigation light is of a specified color and must shine through a prescribed arc, measured in points, i.e., intervals of 11¼ degrees of a circle. Sidelights *(top)* are red to port and green to starboard and shine through 10 points—from dead ahead to two points abaft the beam. Stern lights are white 12-point lights; forward-shining range lights are white 20-point lights, and the all-round white range light shines through 32 points.

Avoiding the Rocks

105

Avoiding the Rocks

International Lights

On the high seas, running lights generally hang higher, are placed farther apart in a ship's rigging and shine more brightly so that they can be seen for much greater distances than the marine lights required by Inland Rules of the Road. The language the lights speak is clear and understandable to any seasoned seaman from Hoboken to Hong Kong—and for good reason: the International Rules were designed primarily to cover large vessels on long and often hazardous voyages, where mistakes can cost millions of dollars or hundreds of lives.

The lighting code in the International Rules takes precedence over all others. That is, when a boat sails from inland to international waters, it must be lighted according to International Rules, but vessels going the other way, into inland waters, need not display lights for Inland Rules. For years only oceangoing vessels and ferryboats were accorded this latter privilege. But in 1940, the Inland Rules were amended to permit all small yachts to maintain International Rules lights when sailing on inland waters.

The lighting regulations for International Rules were also amended in 1948, to accommodate small boats. For those small motorboats that cannot be fitted with lights to conform with the prescribed patterns, the international code now has less stringent rules plus an optional system of lights for a sailboat. These are explained in the illustrations on this page.

An Option in Sidelights

The owner of a sailboat under 40 feet may, under International Rules, dispense with fixed sidelights and equip his boat instead with a half-red, half-green lantern to be fixed in the bow or at least kept ready for immediate use.

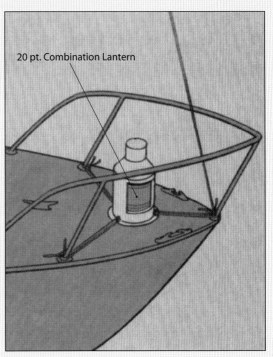

20 pt. Combination Lantern

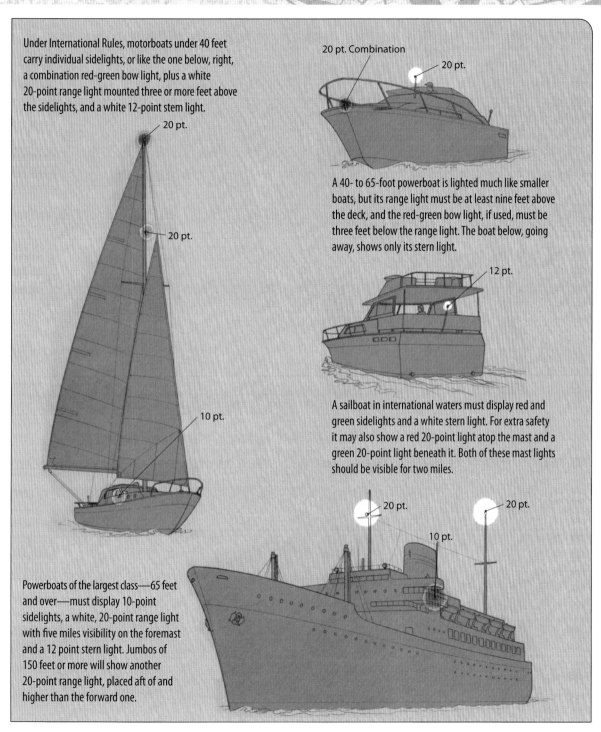

Under International Rules, motorboats under 40 feet carry individual sidelights, or like the one below, right, a combination red-green bow light, plus a white 20-point range light mounted three or more feet above the sidelights, and a white 12-point stem light.

20 pt. Combination

20 pt.

20 pt.

20 pt.

10 pt.

A 40- to 65-foot powerboat is lighted much like smaller boats, but its range light must be at least nine feet above the deck, and the red-green bow light, if used, must be three feet below the range light. The boat below, going away, shows only its stern light.

12 pt.

A sailboat in international waters must display red and green sidelights and a white stern light. For extra safety it may also show a red 20-point light atop the mast and a green 20-point light beneath it. Both of these mast lights should be visible for two miles.

20 pt.

20 pt.

10 pt.

Powerboats of the largest class—65 feet and over—must display 10-point sidelights, a white, 20-point range light with five miles visibility on the foremast and a 12 point stern light. Jumbos of 150 feet or more will show another 20-point range light, placed aft of and higher than the forward one.

Avoiding the Rocks

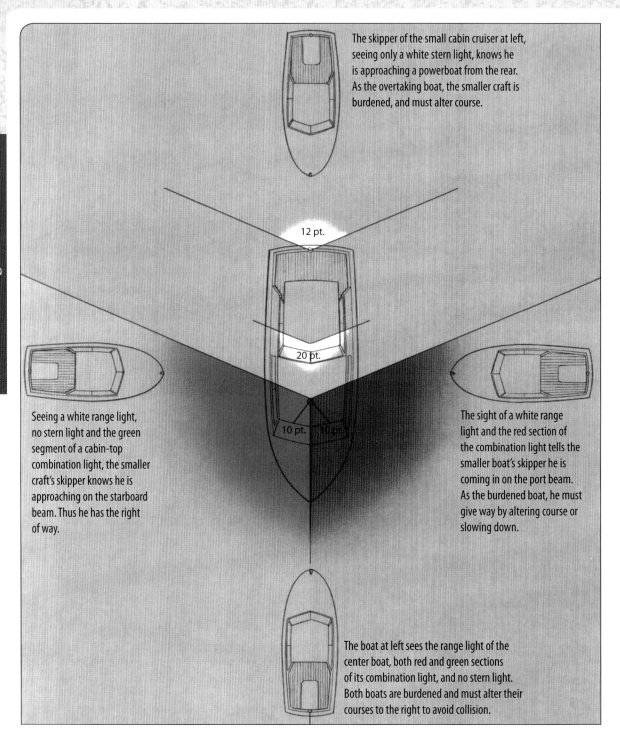

The skipper of the small cabin cruiser at left, seeing only a white stern light, knows he is approaching a powerboat from the rear. As the overtaking boat, the smaller craft is burdened, and must alter course.

12 pt.

20 pt.

10 pt.   10 pt.

Seeing a white range light, no stern light and the green segment of a cabin-top combination light, the smaller craft's skipper knows he is approaching on the starboard beam. Thus he has the right of way.

The sight of a white range light and the red section of the combination light tells the smaller boat's skipper he is coming in on the port beam. As the burdened boat, he must give way by altering course or slowing down.

The boat at left sees the range light of the center boat, both red and green sections of its combination light, and no stern light. Both boats are burdened and must alter their courses to the right to avoid collision.

Changing Look of Lights

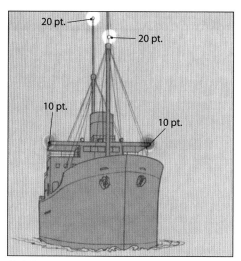

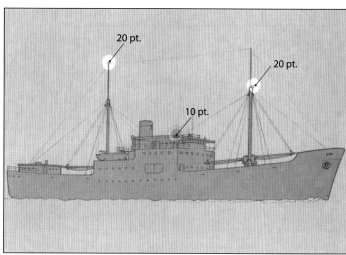

The light patterns on the craft above, lighted under International Rules, show it to be approaching. The vessel's green and red sidelights show simultaneously only when the vessel is viewed head-on. Similarly the white range lights on its masts appear in proximity only when seen from ahead.

As the vessel turns, a stationary observer sees the range lights separate; the red *(port)* sidelight vanishes while the green *(starboard)* sidelight continues to show. This situation, together with the fact that her higher, after range light is on the left, indicates that the vessel is now moving from left to right.

As the ship continues to turn, its 20-point range lights and its 10-point, starboard sidelight—all visible for only two points abaft the beam—vanish. The 12-point white stern light, visible only when the others cannot be seen, has appeared, a sure sign that the vessel is now heading away.

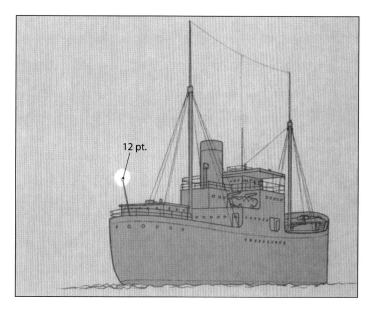

Inland Fishing and Towing

On inland waters, a tug towing one or more barges astern can be recognized by a 20-point forward light, 10-point sidelights and, on the aftermast, three 32-point white lights, set vertically, three feet apart. The first barge has 10-point sidelights and a white light aft (not visible from this angle); the List barge shows two 32-point white lights side by side and 10-point sidelights forward.

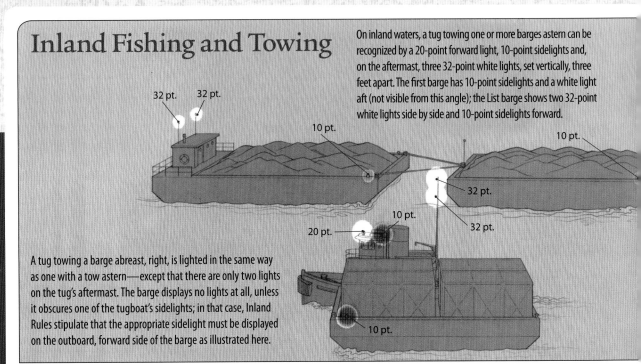

A tug towing a barge abreast, right, is lighted in the same way as one with a tow astern—except that there are only two lights on the tug's aftermast. The barge displays no lights at all, unless it obscures one of the tugboat's sidelights; in that case, Inland Rules stipulate that the appropriate sidelight must be displayed on the outboard, forward side of the barge as illustrated here.

Offshore Fishing and Towing

Vessels towing *(below)* must show 10-point sidelights and a stern light; and on tugs over 150 feet long, a range light on the aftermast. If the tow is less than 600 feet, two white 20-point lights are placed vertically on the tug's foremast. (Three vertical lights mark a tow of more than 600 feet.) The towed boat shows the usual sidelights and a stem light.

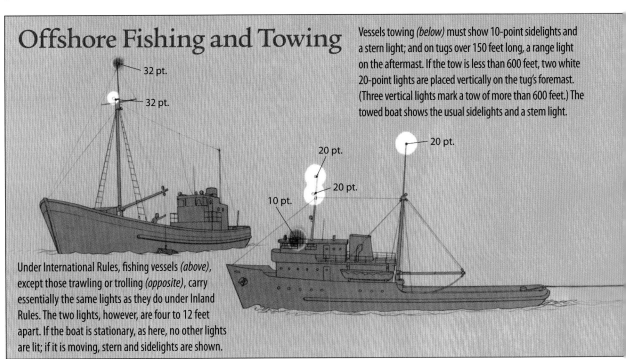

Under International Rules, fishing vessels *(above)*, except those trawling or trolling *(opposite)*, carry essentially the same lights as they do under Inland Rules. The two lights, however, are four to 12 feet apart. If the boat is stationary, as here, no other lights are lit; if it is moving, stern and sidelights are shown.

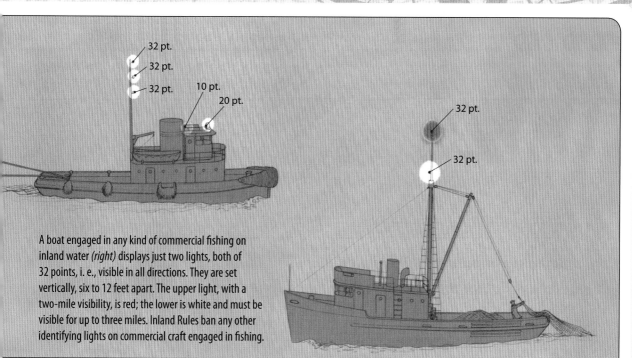

32 pt.
32 pt.
32 pt.
10 pt.
20 pt.
32 pt.
32 pt.

A boat engaged in any kind of commercial fishing on inland water *(right)* displays just two lights, both of 32 points, i. e., visible in all directions. They are set vertically, six to 12 feet apart. The upper light, with a two-mile visibility, is red; the lower is white and must be visible for up to three miles. Inland Rules ban any other identifying lights on commercial craft engaged in fishing.

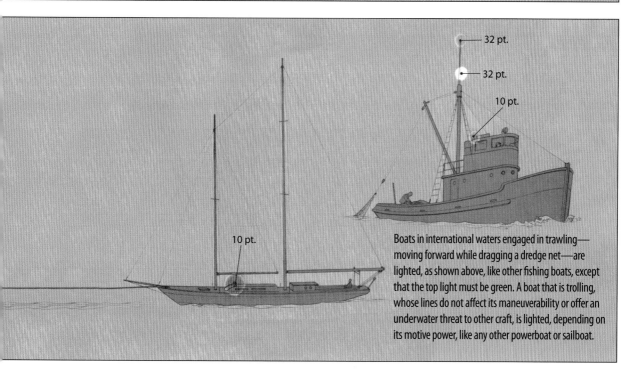

32 pt.
32 pt.
10 pt.
10 pt.

Boats in international waters engaged in trawling—moving forward while dragging a dredge net—are lighted, as shown above, like other fishing boats, except that the top light must be green. A boat that is trolling, whose lines do not affect its maneuverability or offer an underwater threat to other craft, is lighted, depending on its motive power, like any other powerboat or sailboat.

Lights for Anchoring and Distress

The International and Inland Rules require anchored vessels under 150 feet long to show a white light visible at night for two miles. A light of this type is shown right, properly displayed high in the forepart of both a small powerboat and a sailboat. Larger ships anchored at night display two white 32-point lights. The forward light must be at least 20 feet above the hull, and the aft, 15 feet below the forward.

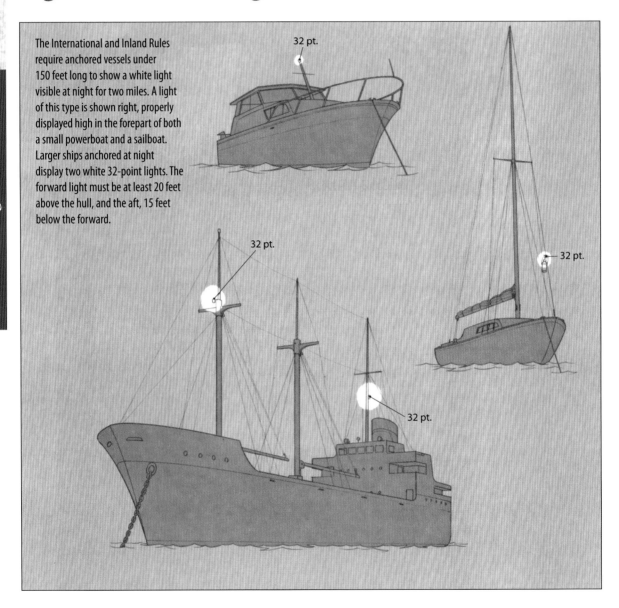

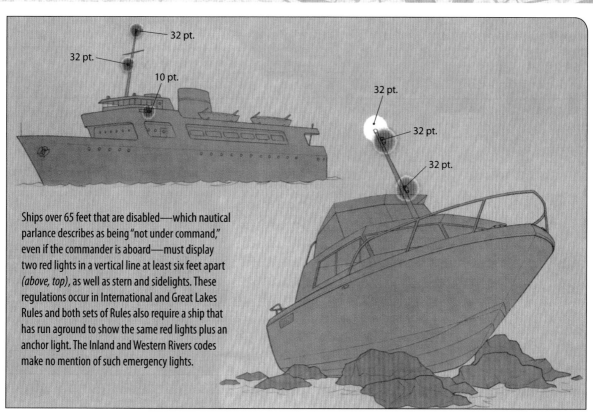

32 pt.

32 pt.

10 pt.

32 pt.

32 pt.

32 pt.

Ships over 65 feet that are disabled—which nautical parlance describes as being "not under command," even if the commander is aboard—must display two red lights in a vertical line at least six feet apart *(above, top)*, as well as stern and sidelights. These regulations occur in International and Great Lakes Rules and both sets of Rules also require a ship that has run aground to show the same red lights plus an anchor light. The Inland and Western Rivers codes make no mention of such emergency lights.

Avoiding the Rocks

An Exception for Side-Wheelers

The Western Rivers Rules have a unique regulation governing the lights of "river steamers," a phrase which defines steam vessels with smokestacks set athwartships. The rule applies to survivors of the Mississippi River's fleet of old side-wheelers. As shown here, a red light on the port stack and a green light on the starboard stack bulge out like frog's eyes and shed 180-degree beams. Like no other sidelights afloat, each can be seen from both ahead and astern.

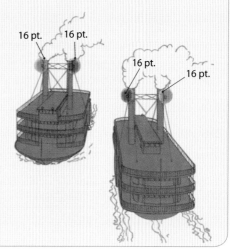

16 pt.   16 pt.

16 pt.

16 pt.

Power and Safety

CHAPTER 4:
Power and Safety

Part of the excitement of boating is the sense of anticipation that wells up as the yachtsman readies his boat to go out on the water. The preparations may involve stepping onto the deck of a 60-foot racing sloop and bending on hundreds of square feet of expensively cut Dacron sails. Getting ready may be as simple as a trip to the gas station to fill up an outboard's portable fuel tank. Or it may entail the most basic boating situation of all—climbing into a rowboat and ferrying away from the dry land to reach a vessel moored in the middle of a harbor. But it makes no difference whether the craft is a six-foot dinghy or a transoceanic yacht—the success of its voyage will depend on the preliminary steps the skipper should take to ensure the safety and well-being of both his boat and its passengers.

The skipper's first preparatory act should be to check the weather. A cardinal rule of boating is that when storm warnings are out, the boat stays in. Boating forecasts often are printed in local newspapers or broadcast by local radio stations—or they may be obtained by phoning the Coast Guard. Moreover, most yacht clubs and marinas fly red pennants when the wind is likely to gust to 30 knots or more, as an advisory to small craft to stay home.

When the mariner is satisfied that the elements are kindly, he should consider the soundness of his boat and its equipment. Do his running lights work? Is his fire extinguisher full and functioning? Does he have a life preserver for each passenger as the law requires? Are these items and all the other gear he needs aboard properly stowed where they will stay in place if a rising sea rocks the boat? Even more important, is he sure that he can get at them in a hurry when needed? Preservers that are inaccessibly squirreled away in the forepeak will save no lives. The skipper should pump out any water that has seeped into the bilge since the last trip and should check for leaks if the bilges seem too full. He might also spend a moment swabbing the deck; dirt and oil spills are slippery and unseamanlike, and they can soil life preservers, sails, and his passengers' best yachting clothes.

Power and Safety

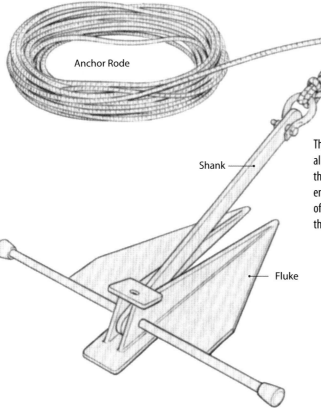

Anchor Rode

Shank

Fluke

The best all-around anchor for small craft is the eight-pound, alloy steel Danforth type shown here. Its twin flukes, hinged to the shank, bite into the bottom—yet fold flat for easy storage. To ensure the flukes a good angle for holding the bottom, the length of the nylon anchor line, called the rode, should be seven times the maximum depth in which the skipper might expect to anchor.

Fuel Safety Check List

The skipper should observe the following safety rules at each fueling.
1. Fill portable tanks off the boat.
2. When fueling fixed tanks, close doors and hatches to keep fumes from collecting in the boat's interior.
3. Keep the fire extinguisher handy.
4. Permit no smoking.
5. Do not operate electrical equipment.
6. Keep the gasoline nozzle in contact with the tank aperture at all times to prevent static sparks.
7. Wipe up spills immediately.
8. Stop fueling before the gas level reaches the top, and replace the cap tightly.
9. After fueling, sniff for fumes and air out the boat thoroughly before starting up the engine.

RULES ON THE WATER

1. No smoking while boat is being fueled.
2. No standing up on small craft that is easily tipped.
3. All children and weak swimmers should wear life jackets as soon as they step on board.

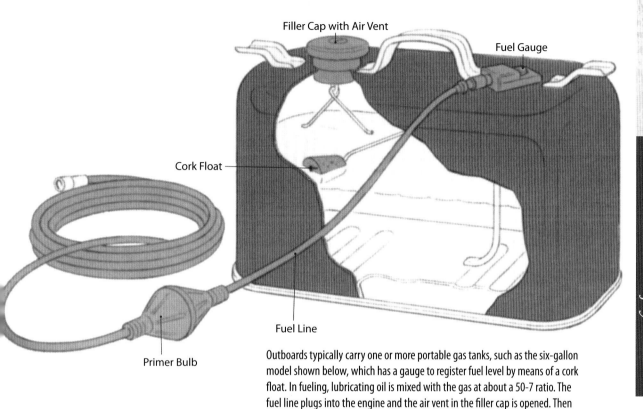

Filler Cap with Air Vent

Fuel Gauge

Cork Float

Fuel Line

Primer Bulb

Power and Safety

Outboards typically carry one or more portable gas tanks, such as the six-gallon model shown below, which has a gauge to register fuel level by means of a cork float. In fueling, lubricating oil is mixed with the gas at about a 50-7 ratio. The fuel line plugs into the engine and the air vent in the filler cap is opened. Then the primer bulb is squeezed to force gas into the carburetor.

Powerboat Preparations

When a powerboat skipper gets ready to take his craft for a spin, the first thing he should do is check out the equipment needed for the trip. Much of the equipment, shown with the typical 19-foot runabout at right, is required by law. This mandatory gear includes a fire extinguisher, a horn or a whistle, and a Coast Guard-approved life jacket for each person on board—plus at least one throwable life-saving device. Since the fuel tanks in the boat shown here are kept in sheltered compartments aft, the compartments are vented, as required, by cowled ducts to carry off gas vapors. For going out after dark, the running-light fitting at the bow shows red to port and green to starboard; the staff on the starboard quarter has a white light at its top.

Beyond these legal necessities, the prudent skipper also carries gear needed to meet any number of manual boat handling situations—as well as occasional breakdowns. Foremost among these articles is a bilge pump for taking out the water shipped aboard in rough weather. There should also be an anchor, ready to be dropped over the side either at some planned destination, or as a safety measure if the boat should start drifting into trouble. Another key item is the owner's manual for the engine, which provides instructions on the care and handling of the power plant; the manual should be accompanied by a tool kit

The runabout's vital equipment is carefully placed to be available when needed. The bow mooring line is run through a chock and cleated. Tool kit and life vests are kept under the seats, and buoyant cushions that double as extra lifesaving gear are quickly accessible. The first-aid kit, bilge pump and paddles are nestled against the starboard side of the hull; the fire extinguisher is within easy reach of the helmsman. Once underway, line and fenders will be stowed forward with the anchor.

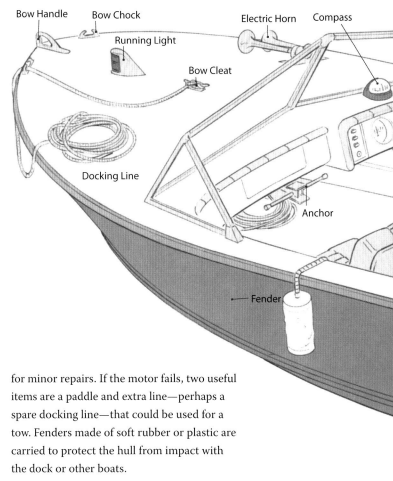

Bow Handle Bow Chock Electric Horn Compass
Running Light
Bow Cleat
Docking Line
Anchor
Fender

for minor repairs. If the motor fails, two useful items are a paddle and extra line—perhaps a spare docking line—that could be used for a tow. Fenders made of soft rubber or plastic are carried to protect the hull from impact with the dock or other boats.

BOATING LESSONS YOU'LL NEVER FORGET

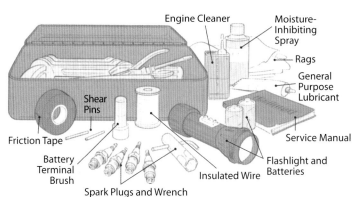

Engine Cleaner
Moisture-Inhibiting Spray
Rags
General Purpose Lubricant
Shear Pins
Friction Tape
Battery Terminal Brush
Spark Plugs and Wrench
Insulated Wire
Service Manual
Flashlight and Batteries

The proper tools for a powerboat's kit must be able to handle repairs ranging from tightening loose wiring and deck fittings to replacing spark plugs and even changing the propeller. Inside the tool box are a set of combination open-end and box wrenches; regular, long-nose and vise-grip pliers; and a hammer, jackknife and assorted nuts, bolts and screws. Ranged around it are spare parts, cleaning and lubricating materials, an aerosol can of spray that dries the engine tor quick starting and a waterproof flashlight.

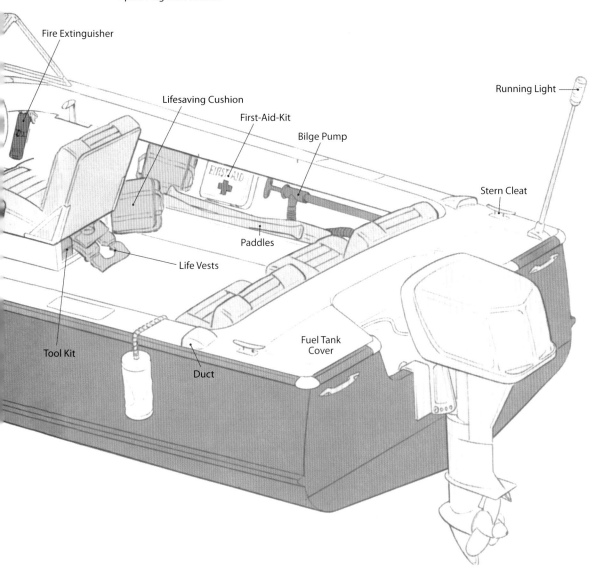

Fire Extinguisher
Lifesaving Cushion
First-Aid-Kit
Bilge Pump
Running Light
Stern Cleat
Paddles
Life Vests
Tool Kit
Duct
Fuel Tank Cover

Essential Safety Gear

Certain general requirements apply in choosing safety gear for any size boat. All boats, for example, must carry Coast Guard-approved life preservers—officially called personal flotation devices, or PFDs. On powerboats, or sailboats with auxiliary engines, fire-fighting gear must also be approved by the Coast Guard, and it should be specifically designed to fight the commonest types of shipboard fires, those fueled by gas, oil, or grease. Sound-making devices for use in fog and for right-of-way signals are required for all boats over 16 feet long.

Carbon Dioxide   Dry Chemical

The two commonest kinds of portable marine fire extinguishers use either carbon dioxide or dry chemicals, both effective for oil or gas fires. Two other Coast Guard-approved types are foam—unpopular with boatmen because of the messy cleanup job afterward—and halon gas, which is a relatively new but effective flame-arresting element.

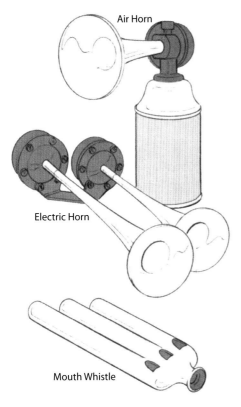

Air Horn

Electric Horn

Mouth Whistle

Both the hand-held Freon air horn and the electric-powered dual horns shown here satisfy the legal requirements for boats up to 65 feet in length. (Boats 26 feet and over must also have a bell.) The whistle, which should be audible for half a mile, meets the rules for boats less than 26 feet in length.

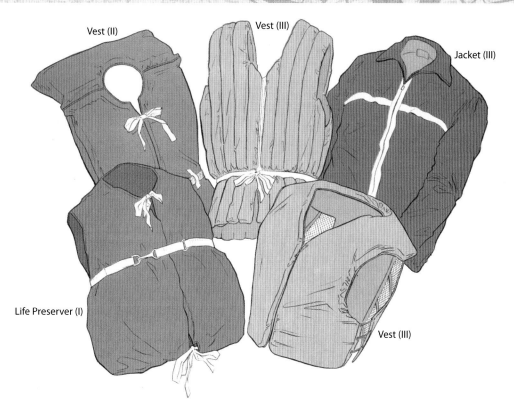

Vest (II)

Vest (III)

Jacket (III)

Life Preserver (I)

Vest (III)

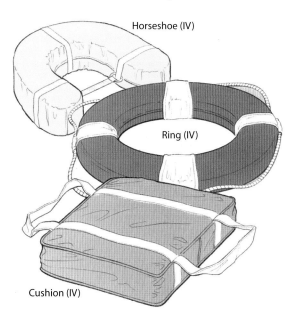

Horseshoe (IV)

Ring (IV)

Cushion (IV)

Personal flotation devices are classed as types I, II and III—the wearables shown at upper right—and type IV, which includes all the throwables above. Boats under 16 feet must carry one of the four types for each occupant, while bigger boats must carry a wearable type for each person, plus at least one throwable. Most recreational boatmen favor type III wearables, either vests or flotation jackets, because they are lighter and more comfortable. Bulkier types I or II, designed to turn an unconscious person face upward in the water, are recommended for commercial and cruising vessels. By law, type I must be orange. Throwable rings 20 inches or more in diameter are also orange—or white. Smaller ones, and all other flotation devices, should be brightly colored for maximum visibility.

Power and Safety

Starting the Engine

The sophisticated motorboats of today start almost as easily as does the family car. A modern inboard, with its automatic choke and self-priming fuel pump, is designed to kick over—and almost always does—whenever the driver hits the starter. After it idles briefly, the skipper can put the engine in gear and go.

The starting system for a standard outboard like the one at right is equally reliable, though the boatman usually has to operate the choke and priming systems by hand. To do so he first opens the air vent on the gas tank and squeezes the primer bulb to force fuel into the carburetor. Then, taking his place at the helm, he pulls out the choke knob to close down the choke, eases the throttle slightly forward and turns the ignition key. When the engine has idled a bit, he moves the choke back to its normal open position, and the boat is ready to leave.

This kind of dependability in starting prevails for virtually all modern boat motors, including the low-horsepower out-boards employed on fishing boats and as sailboat auxiliaries. These are started by pulling a cord that spins the flywheel.

However, there are occasions when any engine may refuse to start. The skipper engages his starter, but the engine merely cranks over without catching—or doesn't crank at all. In such cases, the boatman usually can pinpoint the problem by going through the step-by-step procedures on page 124. Some special tips for inboard starting appear below.

The majority of the time the engine will start running as the operator goes through this sequence of checks. And if the electric starting system on any outboard fails, he can always remove the engine cover, find the rope starter that is included for such emergencies, and crank by hand.

Tips for Inboards

The most frequent starting failures on inboards are due to wet ignition components.
- Open the engine compartment and air it out.
- Dry off plugs, wiring, and terminals with a cloth or by spraying them with a drying agent from an aerosol can.

Another problem can be that the engine is flooded.
- Hit the starter and crank the engine with the throttle wide open. After the engine starts, the throttle is pulled back to idle.

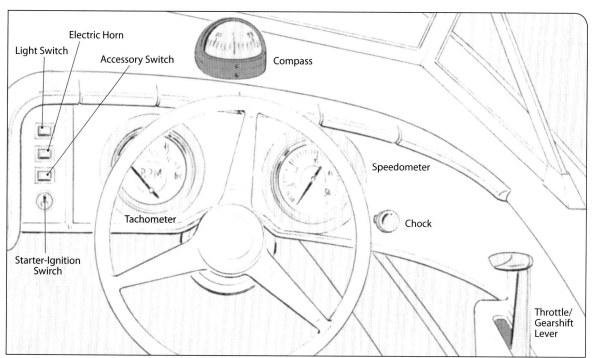

Light Switch
Electric Horn
Accessory Switch
Compass
Speedometer
Tachometer
Chock
Starter-Ignition Swirch
Throttle/ Gearshift Lever

Remote controls for starting a modern outboard motor include a starter-ignition switch, a choke knob that pulls out for starting a cold engine, and a combination throttle-gearshift lever. The dashboard of this boat also has a fitting for a compass, a speedometer, and a tachometer to register rpm's, indicating how efficiently and economically the engine is performing. At far left, a row of buttons includes switches for the horns and for the bow and stern lights.

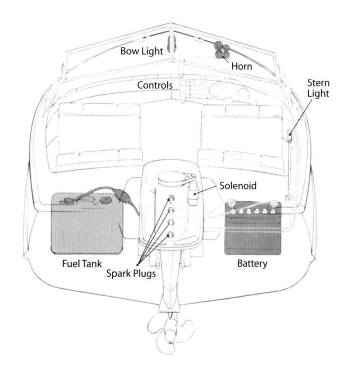

Bow Light
Horn
Controls
Stern Light
Solenoid
Fuel Tank
Spark Plugs
Battery

The electrical system, outlined in blue above, goes to work as the helmsman engages the dashboard starter switch, drawing current from the 12-volt battery and sending it to the starter solenoid. Essentially a relay, the solenoid links the battery and engine via heavy cables that can convey far greater amounts of power than the thin wires leading to and from the dashboard starter switch. When activated, the solenoid conducts power directly from the battery to the starter motor, which will turn the engine over and start it, provided that the gas tank has been fueled and the primer bulb squeezed.

Power and Safety

What to do when the Engine will not Start

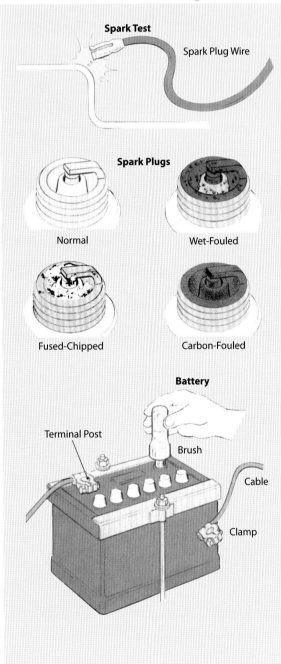

Spark Test

Spark Plug Wire

Spark Plugs

Normal

Wet-Fouled

Fused-Chipped

Carbon-Fouled

Battery

Terminal Post

Brush

Cable

Clamp

Engine Cranks Over without Starting

1. Inspect the fuel supply, and be sure the tank's air vent is open; squeeze the primer bulb to guarantee that the carburetor is full. Set the choke properly: on a cold engine the knob is pulled out all the way to close the choke and enrich the fuel mixture. If the engine is warm, having been recently shut down, the choke knob should be pushed all the way forward, in its normal position.

2. After several futile starting attempts, engine cylinders may become so wet with fuel that combustion cannot occur. The engine is flooded. To clear it, open the choke, set the throttle full ahead and hit the starter. If the engine starts, leave the choke open and pull the throttle back to idle.

3. If the engine still does not start, test the spark and the spark plugs. First, remove the engine cover and make sure that the wires are firmly attached to the plugs and that they are dry. If they are wet, wipe them off or spray them with a drying agent available in an aerosol spray can. Then test the spark by removing one wire from a plug and holding the terminal about a quarter inch from the motor, as shown at left. Press the starter button; sparks should leap between the terminal and the metal. If there is no spark, the trouble is probably somewhere in the engine's wiring circuit, a problem that calls for expert help.

   If there is a spark, remove all wires, unscrew the plugs and inspect the electrode points at their bases. A clean, functioning plug is illustrated at left along with three troublemakers. Points fouled with oil or carbon can be sanded or brushed clean; plugs with fused or damaged points should be replaced. Before putting the plugs back in, clear excess fuel from the engine by cranking it; this will prevent flooding. While cranking, ground the spark plug to the metal of the engine. Otherwise, voltage generated by the ignition system could build up and cause severe damage. With plugs and wires back in place, try the starter again. If the engine does not kick over now, it is time to call a mechanic.

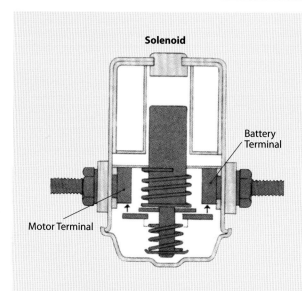

Solenoid

Battery Terminal

Motor Terminal

Starter Is Engaged and Nothing Happens

1. Make sure the battery cables are firmly clamped at the battery and engine terminals. Then try the light switch—if the lights are dim or out, the battery may be weak or dead. If the lights are bright, leave them on and hit the starter again. If the lights dim now, the problem may be a weak battery or bad terminal connections. Remove the cables and clean the terminals and clamps with sandpaper, steel wool or a steel brush such as the one shown at left; then firmly reclamp the cables to the battery.

2. If the battery appears adequately charged and the terminal connections are clean and tight, the problem could be in the starter solenoid, shown at lower left. When the dashboard starter switch is engaged, the central shaft of the solenoid should lift, putting the disc on the lower part of the shaft in contact with the internal terminals for the battery and engine. When this happens there should be an audible click from the solenoid. If there is no click, the solenoid is not working either because it is defective or because of bad wiring between it and the dashboard switch.

3. A defective solenoid must be replaced, but before calling a mechanic, give the wiring system a quick final check. With the ignition off begin at the dashboard starter switch and trace back toward the engine, looking for loose, frayed or damaged wires that may have broken the flow of current.

Power and Safety

Preparing a Sailboat

Power and Safety

The sailboat skipper, like the powerboat-man, should preface every trip by checking his gear. His craft carries many of the same items needed on an outboard, such as a paddle, an anchor and rode, extra line for docking or being towed, life preservers and a first-aid kit. The sailor's repair kit, however, should include line, tape and tools for mending sails and rigging. For rough-weather sailing, he should have a bucket to backstop his bilge pump.

The careful distribution of equipment on the craft above allows for easy accessibility, while at the same time keeping the deck and cockpit uncluttered for handling the boat under sail. Vest-type life preservers, sails, extra line, anchor and rode, along with the tool kit and spinnaker pole are stowed away in the small cabin, or cuddy. A bucket is carried next to a paddle and bilge pump under the seats. Atop the seats are throwable cushions that double as lifesavers.

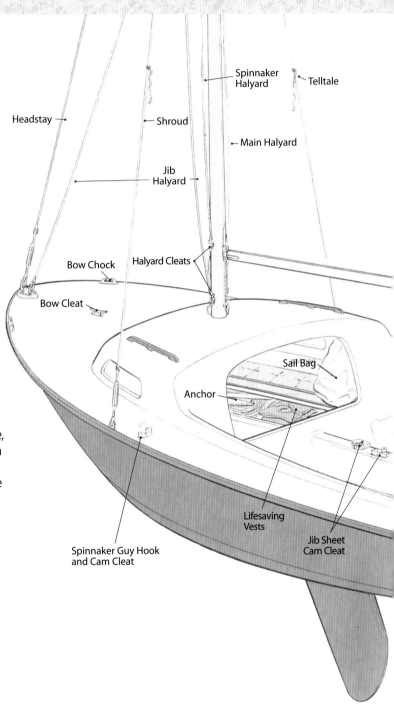

Spinnaker Halyard

Telltale

Headstay

Shroud

Main Halyard

Jib Halyard

Bow Chock

Halyard Cleats

Bow Cleat

Sail Bag

Anchor

Lifesaving Vests

Jib Sheet Cam Cleat

Spinnaker Guy Hook and Cam Cleat

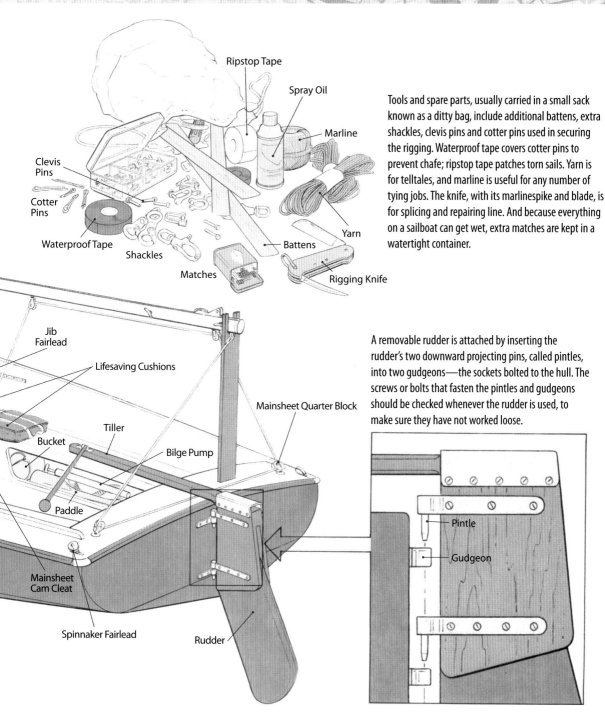

Ripstop Tape

Spray Oil

Marline

Clevis Pins

Cotter Pins

Waterproof Tape

Shackles

Matches

Battens

Yarn

Rigging Knife

Tools and spare parts, usually carried in a small sack known as a ditty bag, include additional battens, extra shackles, clevis pins and cotter pins used in securing the rigging. Waterproof tape covers cotter pins to prevent chafe; ripstop tape patches torn sails. Yarn is for telltales, and marline is useful for any number of tying jobs. The knife, with its marlinespike and blade, is for splicing and repairing line. And because everything on a sailboat can get wet, extra matches are kept in a watertight container.

Jib Fairlead

Lifesaving Cushions

Mainsheet Quarter Block

Tiller

Bucket

Bilge Pump

Paddle

Mainsheet Cam Cleat

Spinnaker Fairlead

Rudder

A removable rudder is attached by inserting the rudder's two downward projecting pins, called pintles, into two gudgeons—the sockets bolted to the hull. The screws or bolts that fasten the pintles and gudgeons should be checked whenever the rudder is used, to make sure they have not worked loose.

Pintle

Gudgeon

Power and Safety

Troubleshooter's Check List

Problem: starter motor works
but engine doesn't

Steps Toward Solution

Power and Safety

Engine not getting fuel	Check the fuel supply. Make sure the fuel-line valve and fuel-tank vent are open. Inspect the fuel line for leakage. Wrap any breaks with tape. Unclog any filters between the fuel supply and the engine. On some inboards, a filter plug can be removed to let sediment drain out. On others the filter must be disassembled and the filtering element cleaned. On outboards, remove the fuel-line assembly from the tank and clean the strainer.
Engine flooded	After letting the engine sit for about half an hour with the ignition off, crank the engine several times with the throttle and the manual choke, if the engine has one, both fully open. Then try restarting the engine.
Engine overheats	Let the engine cool before restarting. If it reheats rapidly, as shown by an inboard's temperature gauge or by heat waves emanating from an outboard, let the engine cool again. Feel around the engine's cooling-water intake and remove any debris clogging it. On inboards, tighten the water-pump belt if it is loose; if it is broken, replace it—with a jury-rigged spare *(opposite)* if necessary. Check the cooling-water hoses for breaks. Check the lubricating oil supply with the dipstick and add oil if necessary. On inboards with closed cooling-water systems, check the tank holding the circulating fresh water and add water if necessary.
Wet or defective wiring	Clean all dirty connections, tighten loose ones, dry off wet ones. Mend or replace loose, broken, frayed or corroded wires, if necessary using a length cut from a less vital part of the boat's electrical system.
Lack of spark	Remove the wire from one spark plug. With the end of the wire one quarter inch from the engine block, crank the engine over. (Or remove the plug, reconnect it to the wire and lay the spark-plug threads against the block.) No spark—or a weak (yellow) one—indicates that repairs must be made in port. A strong (blue) spark means the ignition system is functioning up to the point where current enters the plugs: check each plug.
Defective spark plugs	Dry the upper tips of the plugs and the wire-end connections. Then try starting the engine. If it still does not start, remove the plugs, clean them if they are fouled; replace any damaged ones.

Problem: Starter does
not work

Steps Toward Solution

Discharged or low battery	Turn off lights or other equipment that may be drawing current. Give the battery 30 minutes to recover. Meanwhile, remove the battery cable connections, clean the posts and connections, and reclamp them firmly together. Check each battery cell. If no water is visible, fill with fresh—and preferably distilled—water. On inboards, tighten the belt from the drive shaft to the alternator if it is loose. If it is broken, replace it.
Defective starter switch	Check all connections for tightness; repair broken wires by drawing together their raw ends and then tightly taping over the repair. Cover with tape any piece of wire or connection that is exposed to moisture.
Defective solenoid	Turn on the starter switch and listen for the distinctive click a solenoid makes when working properly. If no click comes, the solenoid is broken, probably beyond the repairing ability of all but a skilled mechanic.

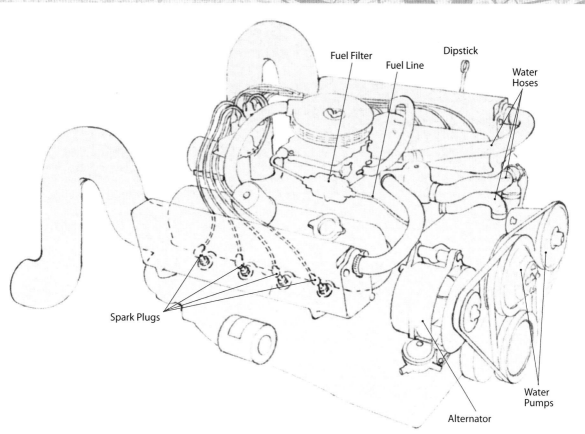

Fuel Filter · Fuel Line · Dipstick · Water Hoses · Spark Plugs · Water Pumps · Alternator

The drawings above show most of the parts of an outboard *(right)* and an inboard engine to which, in case of a breakdown, the average boatman can apply the emergency remedies outlined on page 124.

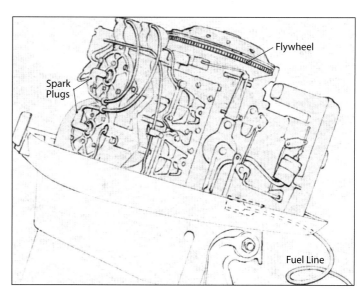

Flywheel · Spark Plugs · Fuel Line

Power and Safety

Power and Safety

Restoring Power

Even the best of marine engines may break down in mid-voyage, and though a trained mechanic may be required for permanent repairs, there are a number of steps a boatman can take to get his motor going long enough to reach port.

By far the commonest cause of marine-engine failure is simply running out of gas. Every skipper should know his engine's average per-hour consumption of gas, and should always top off his tanks before leaving the dock.

The next most common cause of break down is clogged fuel lines, and after that ignition problems, both of which can usually be cured with a spark-plug wrench or one of the other tools and spare parts shown on page 119.

Patience and poise also help. When the engine fails, turn off the ignition and pocket the key to preclude accidental starts or shocks from live wires. Instead of working in haste—or panic—while the boat drifts toward a reef, drop the anchor and take time for careful repairs. Let the engine cool; overheating may be the basic problem, and a cool engine is easier and safer to work on than a hot one. Water slopping aboard onto a hot engine can crack a block; fuel spilled on it can cause an explosion or a fire or both.

Outboard engines, being simpler than inboards, tend to have fewer kinds of problems, but, as the chart of checkpoints for engine troubles *(page 128)* indicates, procedures for tracing the trouble and restoring power are the same for both.

First remove an outboard engine's cover or an inboard's hatch cover. Often the trouble will be quickly apparent—a loose

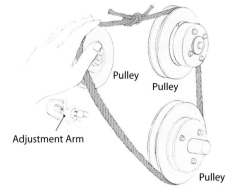

In a pinch, a length of line can be made to substitute for a broken belt on an inboard engine. First loosen the adjusting arm located next to one of the pulleys on which the belt is mounted. Tie the line around the pulleys with a square knot, then retighten the adjusting arm, making the jury-rigged belt as tight as possible. The substitute belt will slip and will soon wear out, but if the engine is run slowly the line may last long enough to get the boat back to port.

wire or a broken belt. Manufacturers even anticipate some of the commonest problems. For example, most outboards will come equipped, in case the electric starter fails, with a manual starter—a cord fitted with a handle and wrapped around a notched collar on the flywheel. If the cord is lost or broken, any light line will serve. A length of line also can substitute for a belt on an inboard engine *(above)*. On most outboards, a damaged propeller *(opposite)* or shear pin can be replaced by a spare. A burst hose can be taped.

Make repairs one careful step at a time. Examine any suspect part. If in doubt about the location or appearance of a part, consult the owner's manual. After completing a repair, put the clutch in neutral before restarting the engine; replace the engine cover before resuming the trip. And if repair is impossible, never be ashamed to signal for help.

To replace a damaged outboard propeller, swing up the lower unit and lock the tilting mechanism. Pull out the cotter pin and unscrew the hub. Remove the gasket behind the hub. Pull off the propeller. Replace the shear pin if it is damaged. Push the new propeller onto the shaft, replace the gasket, and screw on the hub until the cotter-pin holes in the hub and shaft are aligned. Replace the pin.

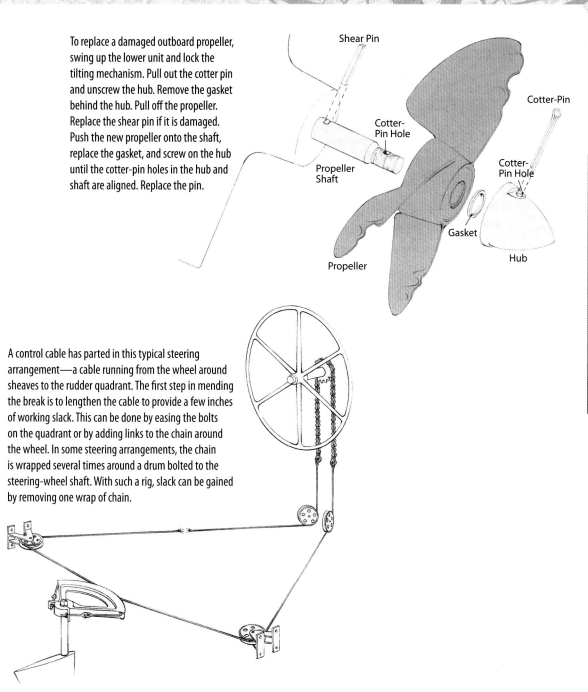

Shear Pin

Cotter-Pin

Cotter-Pin Hole

Cotter-Pin Hole

Propeller Shaft

Gasket

Hub

Propeller

A control cable has parted in this typical steering arrangement—a cable running from the wheel around sheaves to the rudder quadrant. The first step in mending the break is to lengthen the cable to provide a few inches of working slack. This can be done by easing the bolts on the quadrant or by adding links to the chain around the wheel. In some steering arrangements, the chain is wrapped several times around a drum bolted to the steering-wheel shaft. With such a rig, slack can be gained by removing one wrap of chain.

Power and Safety

131

Power and Safety

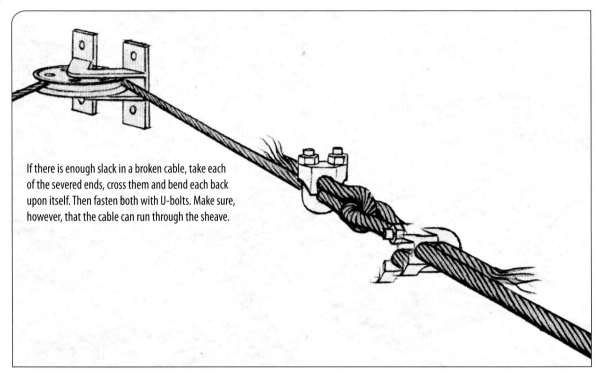

If there is enough slack in a broken cable, take each of the severed ends, cross them and bend each back upon itself. Then fasten both with U-bolts. Make sure, however, that the cable can run through the sheave.

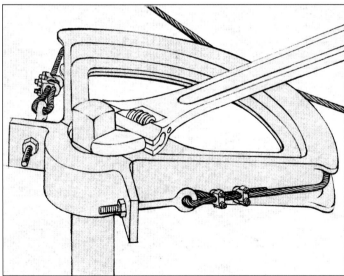

If there is no available slack in the cable, fix a wrench to the rudderhead and use it for a jury tiller. If the wrench is too short, it is often possible to rig a block and tackle to it to provide extra leverage.

Steering Failure

Loss of steering is one of boating's most unnerving emergencies. When it occurs, the skipper, if running on power, should put his engine into neutral. If under sail, he should head into the wind. His object is to slow the boat until he can assess the trouble and devise a solution.

With luck, he will find the rudder intact, with damage done only to the tiller, or in more complex steering mechanisms, to the cable and pulleys that connect the wheel to the rudder. A spare tiller should always be carried on any boat. If it is broken or missing, the crew can fashion a temporary tiller or make the other running repairs shown at left. And if the rudder itself has gone, an ingenious boatman can rig a jury rudder of one kind or another.

One additional recourse is available to a skillful sailboat crew that is denied to those on a powerboat: they can steer with their sails alone, alternately trimming and slacking the jib and main to move the bow onto or off the wind. In a transatlantic race in 1963, the crew of the 58-foot yawl *Dyna* did just that. Early in the race the boat lost its rudder in heavy seas, but the crew sailed on for 1,000 miles, steering by skillful sail handling alone.

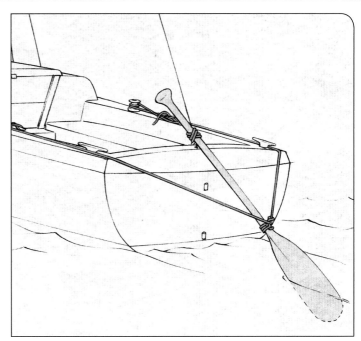

To rig a jury rudder with an oar, form a steering bridle by tying a line around the oar as close as possible to the blade, using a rolling hitch secured with a half hitch. Cleat the ends of the bridle to either side of the boat. Place the oar as far out as possible to increase leverage and lash it to the backstay. The bridle, which should be kept taut by pressure on the oar, can now be trimmed to set direction.

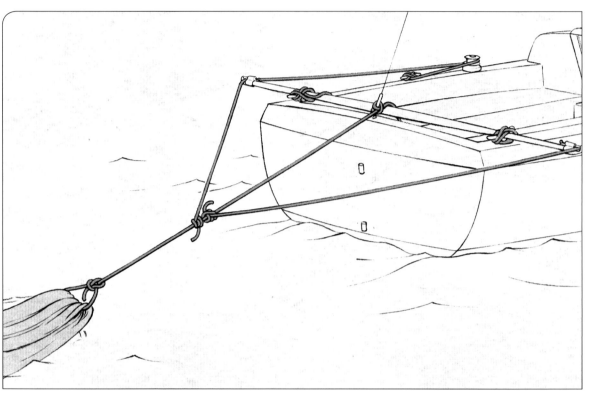

Power and Safety

For an alternate emergency steering gear, a drag—a tire, sea anchor, or *(as here)* a sail—will provide a measure of control. Attach the drag to the stern with a line. Using rolling hitches, tie two other lines to the first, and lead them round a spinnaker pole. Lash the pole across the stern, cleat the two lines, throw the drag out, and trim as required.

Repairing the Rig

Aboard a well-maintained sailboat, the rigging rarely fails. But if it does, the effect may range from the mere inconvenience of a parted sheet to disastrous damage to the standing rigging. Under sail, if a shroud or a stay begins to go, immediately turn the boat so the force of wind on the sails is shifted to undamaged rigging. A weak port shroud, for example, can be kept from parting by putting the boat on the starboard tack. And if the shroud has already broken, prompt action may save the mast.

When standing rigging fails, it must be repaired at once. The simplified drawing on this page shows two methods for fixing a severed stay; either would work just as well on a shroud. The opposite page shows one way to jury-rig after a dismasting. But there is no single "right" way to jury-rig; a spinnaker pole, rather than an oar, might serve as a temporary mast. The seaman must improvise a rig, using available materials, so that he can hoist a sail.

If a stay breaks within a crewman's reach, he can repair it with a handy-billy, as has been done with the headstay above. To make this repair, the instant the stay lets go, turn the boat directly downwind, taking all forward strain off the mast. Leave the main up with the boom well out. Rig an extra jib or spinnaker halyard as a temporary headstay. Then let the jib down; make a loop in each of the stay's severed ends and secure them with U-bolts. After joining the loops with a handy-billy—and using it to pull the stay up tight—rehoist the jib.

A temporary stay can be made of a halyard—shown here replacing the backstay. When the backstay parts, immediately head into the wind so that the wind's force presses aft on the mast. Quickly sheet the boom hard amidships; this causes the mainsail leech to act with the sheet as a temporary backstay. Then tighten the topping lift to provide additional staying force. After lowering the jib and the main, shackle the main halyard to the backstay chain plate and pull the halyard tight with its winch. When the jury-rig is set up, the crew can hoist the main with the jib halyard to get underway again.

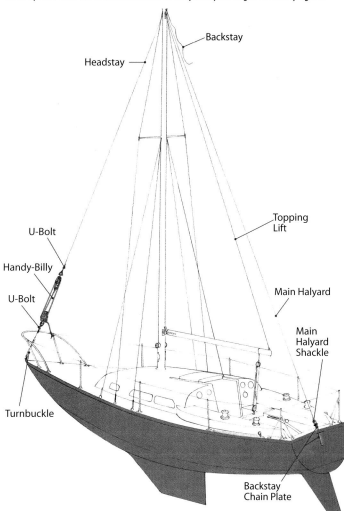

Backstay

Headstay

Topping Lift

U-Bolt

Handy-Billy

U-Bolt

Main Halyard

Main Halyard Shackle

Turnbuckle

Backstay Chain Plate

Power and Safety

Power and Safety

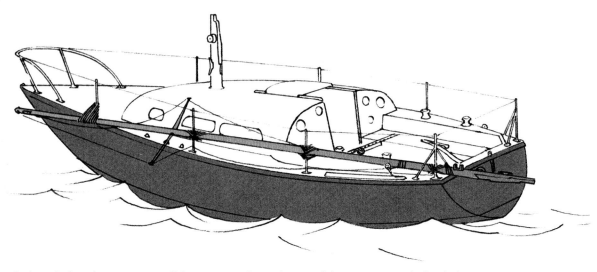

The first task after a dismasting—once all the crew is accounted for—is to get control of the broken spar so it cannot punch through the hull. In a moderate sea, the crew may be able to lash the mast tightly to the deck *(top)*. In rough water, the entire rig must be cast away to prevent hull damage. Wire shrouds and stays, frequently too tough for wire cutters, can be detached at the turnbuckles. Though a wood mast tends to break completely, remnants of an aluminum mast may have to be sheared off with wire cutters or a hacksaw. Try to salvage sheets and halyards; they are invaluable for jury-rigging.

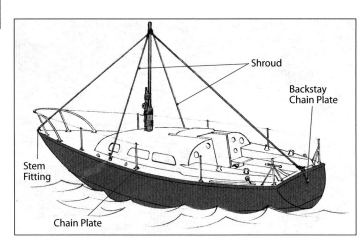

Stem Fitting

Shroud

Backstay Chain Plate

Chain Plate

A new mast can be rigged from an oar secured by shrouds and stays made from jib or spinnaker lines. After cutting four lengths of line, tie one end of each to the oar handle with a clove hitch secured by a half hitch. Then lash the oar to the stump of the mast. Reeve the new shrouds through the chain plates on deck, using shackles if necessary to prevent chafing, and adjust the shrouds to hold the oar vertical. Fasten the headstay to the stem fitting (or to a mooring cleat), then pass the backstay through the stern chain plate and tighten it to keep the oar upright.

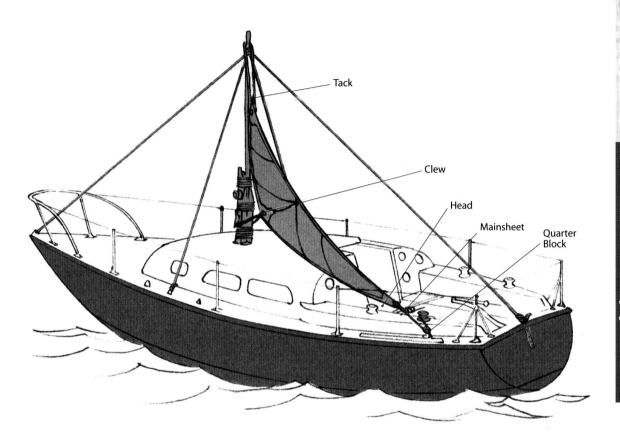

While almost any small sail can be bent to the new mast, the best sail to use is the heavy-duty storm jib, whose foot becomes the luff in the new rig. Tie the tack of the jib (now the head) to the mast above the shrouds and stays so it will not slide down. Fasten the clew (now the tack) to the base of the mast below a cleat, or with several turns of line, to keep the sail from riding up. Then attach the mainsheet to the head of the jib (now the clew), reeve it through the quarter block and take it around a winch to trim the sail.

Aid for an Upset

A powerboat skipper who spots an overturned craft like the sailing dinghy at right should always investigate to see if he can help. Often, the sailboat's crew will be able to cope alone; but sometimes, even if they seem to be righting the boat, heavy winds or waves may make it impossible for the sailors to keep it upright long enough to bail it out. Sails and rigging may be damaged or tangled beyond the crew's ability to get the craft moving again.

Whatever the circumstances, the seagoing Samaritan should approach the situation cautiously. In any rescue operation, and especially one involving people in the water, an enthusiastic but careless rescuer can do more harm than good. He should first hail those in the water to make sure they want his help; if so, he should slowly nose up to the capsized craft from downwind. As soon as he is at the scene, he should shut off his engine; not only is a turning propeller a menace to people in the water, but it can easily be fouled and immobilized by the various lines—sheets, halyards or painter—that are bound to be trailing in the water from the overturned sailboat. Using the rescue boat as a platform, all hands can concentrate on getting the capsized vessel upright, bailed out, and ready to resume operations.

In many cases, however, a craft so stricken may be in no condition to continue sailing, or its sodden crew members may be in bad shape themselves. In such circumstances, the rescuer should stand ready to supply one final good turn—a tow back to port.

Approaching a capsized sailing dinghy, the skipper of a small outboard *(above)* comes close enough to size up the situation and to ask the victims of the upset if he can be of any help. Given an affirmative answer, he takes a gingerly course to leeward so that he can make an upwind approach and avoid being blown into the dinghy or the men clinging to it. When he is a few yards downwind of the victims, the skipper should cut his engine and coast up alongside.

Using the powerboat as a platform, the three men right the dinghy *(above)*, whose rigging has become so snarled that the sail cannot be lowered. The rescuer uses his bilge pump to help bail the water-filled craft while one sailor holds the dinghy alongside. The other sailor, still in the water, steadies the dinghy with one hand and bails with the other.

Since the dinghy can't be sailed home, the rescuer sets out to tow it with a line from the dinghy's bow eye made fast to the powerboat's stern cleat. The tangled mainsail has been detached from the boom so it will not fill with wind. One sailor rides in the towboat, watching the towline; the other stays aboard the dinghy to steer, keeping his weight well aft to prevent the bow from digging into the water and slewing the craft.

Index

c: chart
i: illustration
p: photo

A

Abandoning ship, 56
Advancing squall line, *p: 34*
Air rescue, 64-67, *i: 64-67*
Alcohol stoves, why fire flare-ups occur, *i: 18*
Anchor, best all-around, *i: 116*
Anchor rode, *i: 116*
Avoiding rocks, 68

B

Bailing water, 49, *i: 49*
Bermuda, 24, 38
Blackbeard Shoal, *i: 81*
Boat, overtaking another, *i: 93*
Boats, crossing, *i: 93*

C

Calling for help, *c: 103*
Cartography
    abbreviations, 82
    coastline, representation of, *c: 84-85*
    landmarks, symbols for, *c: 86, 87*
    matching symbols to landmarks, *i:/p: 88-89*
        signposts, ecumenical, *c: 87*
        symbols used, 82
Charts, role in navigation, *i: 78*
China Sea, 8
Cirrus clouds, *p: 32*
Cirroculumus clouds, *p: 32*
Cirrostratus clouds, *p: 33*
Cleats, quick action
    jam cleat, 10
    cam cleat, 10

Clouds
    cirrus, *p: 32*
    cirrocumulus, p*i: 32*
    cirrostratus, *p: 33*
    cumulus, *p: 33*
    height of, *c: 33*
    stratus *p: 32*
    types of, *c: 32-33*
Coast, appearance on maps, *c: 84-85*
Coast Guard Pilot Rules, 100
Coils
    halyard, 11
    sea gasket, 11
    stowing, 11
Cold front, *i: 29*
Collisions, of powerboats, avoiding, *i: 92*
Collisions, of sailboats, avoiding, *i: 94*
Come about, *i: 40*
Cumulus clouds, *p: 33*

D

Distress flag, *i: 55*

E

Engine
    inboard, *i: 129*
    outboard, *i: 129*
    restoring power, 130-131, *i: 131-132*
Engine fires, how to fight, *i: 22-23*
Explosion hatch, *i: 23*
Exterior patch, how to, *i: 46*

F

Fairway, intrusions, *i: 97*

Fire extinguishers, locating, *i: 17*; types of, 16
    foam, how to use, *i: 22*

Fire, in galley, *i: 18-18*

Firefighters, checklist for, 16

Fires, fighting on board, 16-22

Fishing boat, shape, *i: 98*

Flares, as distress signal, how to use, *i: 54*

Fog signals, *c: 101*

Fog and distress signals, 102

Fuel tank, ventilation, set up, *i: 23*

G

Galway Blazer II, 44, *i: 44-46*

GPS units, *i: 52*

H

Halyard coil, how to tie, *i: 11*

Help, signaling for, 50, *i: 50*

Hurricane, riding out, 24

I

Inland fishing and towing, *i: 110-111*

Interior patch, *i: 46*

International Rules for boating, 101

J

Jibe, i: 40

K

King, William, 44-46

L

Land sea breeze systems, 12-13, *i: 12-13*

Lights, for anchoring and distress, *i: 112-113*

Lights, international, rules for, 106, *i: 106-109*

Lights, meaning of, on inland waters, *i: 104-105*

Liquid petroleum gas stove, set up, *i: 19*; tanks for, *i: 19*

Log book, *i: 52*

Lost at sea, 70

Lucette, 56, *i: 57-61*

M

Maine, coast, water depth chart, *i: 80*

Man overboard, 38
    re-entering the boat, *i: 41*
    rescuing from water, *i: 41*
    search and pickup, 40, *i: 40*

N

Newport, Rhode Island, 24

Index

Index

O

Offshore fishing and towing, *i: 110-111*

Offshore winds, 14, *i: 14*

Onshore winds, 14, *i: 14*

Outboard motors, fuel for, *i: 117*

Overturned boat, assisting, how to, 138; *p: 138-139*

P

Pentland Firth, 36

Powerboat engine, starting, 122

    electrical system, 123

    remote controls, 123

    restoring power, 130-131, *i: 131-132*

    tips, 122

    troubleshooting, 124-125, *c: 128*

Powerboats, equipment needed, 118, *i: 118-119*

Powerboats, right-of-way rules, *i: 99*

Powerboats, safety gear for, 120, *i: 120-121*

R

Radio distress calls, 51-53

    alphabet for, 53

    making, 51

    rules for, 53

Raft, as refuge, 62, *i: 62-63*

Rig, parts of, *i: 135-137*

    repairing, how to, 135, *i: 135-137*

Robertson, Dougal, 56, *i: 57-61*

Rocks, avoiding, 68

Rules, while on water, 116

S

Sailboat, preparing, 126; *i: 126-127*

Sailboat, right of way, *i: 95-96*

Samuel Pepys, 24

Santa Cruz Harbor, Monterey Bay, California, *i:/p: 88-89*

Scylla, 38Sea gasket coil, how to tie, 11

Shark attack, 44, *i: 44-45*

Signaling distress, devices for, *i: 103*

Signaling for help, 50, *i: 50*

Spare parts, importance of having, *i: 49*

Squall line, advancing, *p: 34*

St. Catherines Sound, Georgia, *c: 83*

St. James Islands, Great and Little, charts, *i: 79*

Steering failure, 133, *i: 133*

    emergency steering, *i: 134*

Storm system, profile of, 35

Stoves

    Alcohol, why flare-ups occur, *i: 18*

    Liquid petroleum gas, set up, *i: 19;* tanks for, *i: 19*

Stowing gear, methods for, *i: 11*

    halyard coil, 11

    sea gasket coil, 11

    stowing coil, 11

Stowing coil, 11

Stratus clouds, *p: 32*

T
Terrain, underwater, 81
Tavy II, 8-9
Thunderstorm, signs of, *p: 34*
Tidal bore, *p: 72*
Tidal current, *p: 71; i: 73*
Tornado, *p: 34*
Typhoon, fleeing, 8-9

W
Warm front, *i: 28*
Warm front occlusion, *i: 29*
Water, bailing, *i: 48*
Waterway courtesy, 90, *p: 90*
Waves, 74; *p: 74-75;* conditions of, *p: 76*
Waves, mountainous, *p: 77*
Weather, how it works, 28-31, *i: 28-31*
Weather, reading, 26
Western Rivers and Great Lakes Rules, for boating, 100
Weston, Jack, *p: 39*
Whales, striking boat, *i: 57-61*
Whirlpool, *p: 71*
Wind patterns, 12-13; *i: 12-13*
Winds, westerly, *i: 30-31*
Wind rose, *i: 12*
Wind shadow, *i: 15*
Winds
    offshore, 14; *i: 14*
    onshore, 14; *i: 14*

Z
Zones of approach, *i: 92*

Index

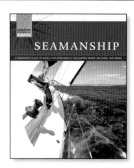

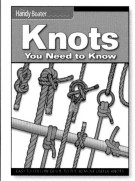
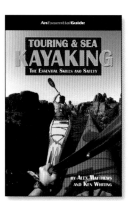